Metalworking
for the
Designer and Technician

Metalworking
for the
Designer
and
Technician

Douglas C. Taylor

41265

DRAMA BOOK SPECIALISTS (PUBLISHERS)
NEW YORK

Library of Congress Cataloging in Publication Data

Taylor, Douglas C.
  Metalworking for the designer and technician.

  Bibliography: p.
  1. Metals in stage setting.   2. Metal-work.
I. Title.
PN2091.M48T3   684'.09'024792   78-23346
ISBN 0-910482-86-1

10 9 8 7 6 5 4 3 2 1

Manufactured in the United States of America

Table of Contents

Acknowledgments

Rod W. Alexander, Director of Theatre, Dartmouth College.
    For starting the project.

David Hale, Chairman, Department of Theatre, Temple University.
    For his constructive criticism and encouragement.

Terry Sateren, Technical Director, The Guthrie Theater.
    Who was most generous with his time, photographs and expertise.

Scene designers Carolyn L. Ross, Daniel Boylen and especially John Jensen.
    Who gave free access to their portfolios, photographs and drawings.

Frederick P. Schleipman, Howarth D. Williams, Jr. and William E. Robbins of the Thayer School Machine Shop.
    Who taught me much and answered innumerable questions.

Stanley LaFountain and Erling Heisted of the Hopkins Center Student Workshop.
    Who answered many questions on blacksmithing and metal-spinning, respectively.

Paul Philbrick, Harold Adams and Raymond Gilman of the Mount Washington Cog Railway Shops.
    Who taught me an awful lot about metal and metalworking.

Leslie Evans, Graphic Artist.
    For her drawings.

The Aluminum Company of America (ALCOA).
    For their materials used in Appendix A.

The American Institute of Steel Construction, Inc.
    For their materials used in Appendices B and C.

The L.S. Starrett Company.
    For their chart used in Appendix D.

Mary M. Taylor.
    For her support and understanding.

Metalworking
for the
Designer and Technician

Introduction

Although the word *metal* no longer inspires open-mouthed awe when it is mentioned for use as stage scenery, many technicians and designers do not know how to use it. Walk through the average scene shop and you will almost never see a trace of flameproof metal in the midst of the stacks of wood and cloth. Students of technical theatre spend hours studying complex knots or techniques of intricate wooden construction but panic at the suggestion that they attempt to weld a simple saddle iron. Most standard scenic texts barely mention any materials other than wood and cloth. In short, metal is still an unknown in many theatres, a feared substance, an alien material.

This need not be the case. Metalworking can be mastered, and without huge inventories of specialized, expensive equipment. The results are well worth the effort. Often the use of such metals as aluminum and steel will solve difficult technical and design problems. Many situations exist where the use of metal is the only answer.

Therefore, I would like to illustrate some of the many possibilities of this different scenic material and explain how to work with it. I will attempt to show how metal can be used within the financial and labor-skill limits of the average theatre shop.

1

Metal and Its Use for the Theatre

Various metals, particularly aluminum and steel, are being used more and more by theatre technicians. Steel is used for simple hardware like hinges, braces and foot irons as well as for sophisticated, well-engineered devices like hydraulically-driven winches. The Guthrie Theater in Minneapolis, for instance, has constructed air-operated scissors elevators, air-castered platforms that use their steel framing as the air distribution system and trap lids that swing down to become their own escape stairs. Even the wooden lift-caster plank has been replaced by a steel hydraulically-operated lift caster. (Any number of these may be placed anywhere under a unit and raised and lowered with one pump. Unlike their wooden predecessors, the casters do not have to be accessible to operate.)

Metal is also useful for much more than stage equipment and theatrical machinery. It may be used for such scenery basics as platforms and even flats. Wood, while useful for decks, is not the best material for platform structure: joints loosen and creak, knots weaken, and long spans require large, heavy and expensive beams for support. Wood requires too much volume to achieve needed strength, and any joint becomes a spot for potential failure.

Air-activated scissors elevator, The Guthrie Theater.

Trap cover that drops to become escape stairs, The Guthrie Theater.

Terry Sateren's hydraulic lift casters and pump, The Guthrie Theater.

Steel can be an excellent alternative platform material. It has strength, and by using adequately braced thin sections (tubing, channel or angle stock) to do the same work as thicker, heavier pieces (solid bar stock), one can produce platforms that are strong and lightweight. For example, a small wagon need only be 1¾" thick on its edge instead of the 6" required with wood, and its caster mountings can be solidly welded into place. Larger units can be framed with 16 gauge 2" square steel tubing. Not only does this produce a strong, light frame, but joints are welded airtight and the frame itself can provide the piping for air-casters or air-operated devices within the unit. Long-span construction can use lightweight steel trusses—either homemade or commercially available. Even simple platform units, like stair-fillers, are best made from steel when one considers the many times they must be placed and removed in the course of a season.

The use of metal, in this case steel, for flat construction is a relatively new approach in the theatre. It is common knowledge that once a flat exceeds 16' in height the standard 1 × 3 becomes inadequate. For years professional theatre has relied on ⁵⁄₄" × 4" C select pine to frame its flats to withstand the heights of design and the rigors of the road. This type of lumber is becoming increasingly expensive and many technical directors are being forced to use the 2 × 4. Although these generally have the required strength, they are usually limited to 16' in length and often warp—given the climatic extremes of frozen lumberyards and superheated stages. Also, they are heavy, particularly when used with a hard cover instead of the lighter, but flapping, canvas. (At times, scenery can be suggestive, but the audience will no longer overlook walls that ripple when a door in the set is slammed.)

To overcome these limitations of the conventional large flat, it is possible to build flats framed from 18 gauge, 1" square steel tubing. The frames

Small, steel tubing framed wagon, The Guthrie Theater.

Platform under construction, The Guthrie Theater.

Large, steel tubing framed wagon, The Guthrie Theater.

Lightweight steel trusses for longspan platforming, The Guthrie Theater.

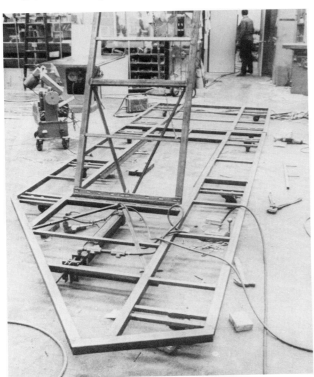

Steel tubing framed ceiling piece, The Guthrie Theater.

are cut to size, welded together by portable MIG units (welders that automatically feed the electrode wire and shield it with inert gas as they weld, cleanly and quickly) and then are covered with ¼" plywood. This cover is attached with self-drilling, self-threading screws driven by power screwdrivers. The surface of the completed flat is then textured in any manner the design requires.

While this may appear to be a heavy, complicated way to build flat scenery, it is not. The steel tubing is lighter than wood framing of the required strength, and the cost is approximately one-half that of the lumber, when purchased in 5,000' lots. Another advantage: this scenery is easily joined and separated, and requires almost no maintenance.

Metal framing is a structurally sound way to create free-form rocks, hills and other three-dimensional shapes. Traditionally, these are framed with ¾" plywood or flat formers and layered with scrap wood, lath, chicken wire, dope and rag to achieve their desired shape. The results are often very heavy, solid structures that creak ominously as actors use them. Steel framing can provide a thin, solid shell of support that does not creak or wiggle.

Metal is too versatile a material to belong solely to the technical director and his or her crews—it is a valuable material for the designer as well. Metal can be used structurally as part of a design, such as steel scaffolding with various scenic accessories bolted onto it. This is a quick, inexpensive way to get a lot of structure, particularly when you rent the scaffolding. There is one drawback, however; scaffolding parts fit together loosely and there may be problems in trying to suppress the clanking. Steel also may appear more strikingly, such as the creation of a skyline from Telespar, a telescoping square tubing that bolts together readily. Telespar also can be welded into simple platforms and intricate stairs.

Round tubing and expanded metal mesh can be used effectively also. Simple jigs are used to

Platform and structure for *Love's Labours Lost*, John Jensen, designer; The Guthrie Theater.

Set for *Guys and Dolls*, John Jensen, designer; Dartmouth College.

Steel tubing framed flats for *Cat On A Hot Tin Roof*, The Guthrie Theater.

Detail of flat-joining hardware, The Guthrie Theater.

Set for *Agamemnon—Homecoming*, Carolyn Ross, designer; Dartmouth College.

Set for *Dr. Faustus*, Ralph Funicello, designer; The Guthrie Theater.

Set for *A Midsummer Night's Dream*, John Jensen, designer; The Guthrie Theater.

Construction detail, *Dr. Faustus*; Terry Sateren, technical director; The Guthrie Theater.

Set for *Indians*, Daniel Boylen, designer; Temple University.

hot-bend curves and, after welding, the unit can be finished with applied fabric decoration. Hydraulically-activated lift-casters can be used to create a main unit that folds at the middle for shifting.

Steel tubing can be bent into free-flowing, fantastic shapes and still provide enough strength for the actor to use it. Tubing also can become very formalized.

Pipe, a readily obtainable material, can be used effectively in exposed-steel designs. Angle stock can be bent to support a circular catwalk above a playing area, for instance.

An excellent use of metal as structure is a channel and large steel tubing supporting flying staircases and a cantilever of a set.

One area of theatre technology and design where metal can play a vital part is railings. Here the use of metal can vary from internal reinforcement and mesh decoration to the strong, practical shape of square tubing railings. Unlike those built from traditional stage materials, metal railings are practical and usable.

Metal may even be used to construct the designer's model of the set. Such a model will endure the rigors of rehearsal, and is most useful in the shop when the actual set is being constructed.

Metal need not *show* in the completed set to be useful to the designer. Square steel tubing can frame flats, structure stairs and platforms and even

Construction detail, *The Tempest*; John Jensen, designer; The Guthrie Theater.

Detail, *A Midsummer Night's Dream*, The Guthrie Theater.

Square tubing railing detail, The Guthrie Theater.

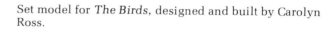

Ship for *The Tempest*, John Jensen, designer; Minnesota Theatre Company.

Set model for *The Birds*, designed and built by Carolyn Ross.

a breakaway wall. You can use metal to your advantage—and the audience never has to know it!

Metal and metalworking can also be useful in the property department. Various personal items are readily crafted from metals like aluminum, steel, copper, brass, lead and magnesium. Elaborate set props can be both aesthetically pleasing and practically strong. Wire and small rods can be soldered together to create all sorts of items—like a flying machine. Furniture can be welded from rod, bar or tubing, or existent pieces can be reinforced with new metal interior supports. Custom-shaped dishes and goblets can be spun out of metal disks. Brass beds, necessary for innumerable productions, can have their cast-iron supports reworked and brazed back together with ease. Dinosaurs can be framed with Telespar and pipe so actors may crawl over them. The possibilities for using metal in prop construction are endless.

Special note should be made regarding the use of metal for stage weapons. Here the main trick is strength and light weight. Aluminum jig plate, which is tempered, is a great material that can be sawed into dull-edged sabers, broadswords and the like. Magnesium, though expensive, is even lighter. Both metals ring satisfyingly when clashed against one another in a stage duel. Large broadswords can be welded together from light sheet steel so that they will have a flattened diamond cross-section. In any

Universe model for *Dr. Faustus*, The Guthrie Theater.

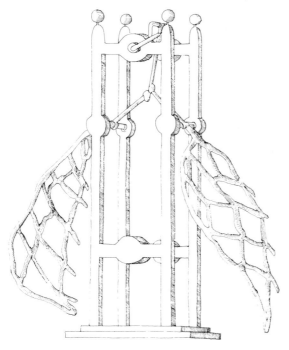

Flying machine, prop; *Dr. Faustus*, The Guthrie Theater.

Set for *The Downstairs Dragon*, Carolyn Ross, designer; Dartmouth College.

case, the weapon is lightweight and if an actor miscalculates, the consequences should be less devastating than those caused by the real thing.

Why use metal for props and scenery?

It can do the job better.

It can save time in doing it.

It can cost less.

It can look better.

2

Metals

The word *metal* is a vague word. If you hunted through the metal supply houses of the world you would be overwhelmed by the fantastic variety of complex alloys or special combinations of about 40 elemental metals. These come in variations of size and shape that defy the imagination.

We need only concern ourselves with a handful of basic metals for most theatrical applications. I have selected five—lead, brass, copper, aluminum and steel—as being most useful to us on a day-to-day basis. Other metals might be useful in specific situations.

What considerations apply when choosing a metal? *Strength*—will it take the stresses and strains of the active theatre? *Workability*—can it be easily shaped and joined in a scene shop? *Cost*—is it affordable? *Other*—does it have a special, distinct property that makes it particularly suitable for theatrical use? Now let us consider the five metals within the framework of these four factors.

Lead

Lead is a bluish-gray, soft, heavy and malleable metal. Weight is lead's most distinguishable factor—about 710 lbs. per cubic foot. It is this great weight in relation to its volume which makes it most useful for theatrical applications: as counterweight bricks, as lineweights and as weights for jacks. Although its strength is low, lead is easily worked; bars and sheets of it may be hammered or bent into the required shape to provide weights for innumerable objects. If the needed shape is too hard to form by these methods, lead can be easily melted and cast. Lead melts at a relatively low 617°F, so the plaster molds and the casting procedure are simple enough for the average scene shop.

A limiting factor in the wide use of lead for general weighting in the theatre is cost—presently $.63 per lb., a small volume. It is available in 5 lb. ingots, as a shredded lead wool and in sheets of varying thicknesses. The cost limits its use to situations where the importance of great weight to low volume is paramount—as in double-speed counterweight systems, or stabilized and counterbalanced properties or electrical fixtures.

Brass

Brass, an alloy of copper and zinc, weighs 534 lbs. per cubic foot. Its excellent strength and wear characteristics make it most useful as a bearing material —often as bushings for sheaves and wheels or shaft bearings for tools and machinery. Although casting brass is well beyond the scope of any shop other than a small foundry, it can be considered readily workable. It is easily machined—drilling, tapping, filing and the like present no major problems, even to the unskilled worker. Likewise, joining is simple. Aside from the usual techniques of bolting, riveting and clamping, brass can be joined by gluing with epoxy, soldering (both hard and soft) and brazing (the process of welding with brass).

Brass is available in wire, round stock, bars, sheets, tubes, pipes and assorted castings and extrusions. Prices depend upon the alloy, amount and shape. Special note should be made that many gears are available in brass. Some could be useful in developing new types of stage mechanisms or tools. Brass and bronze bushings for bearings are readily available.

Brass often turns up in properties which the technician must repair or alter. Candlesticks, cooking wares, beds, decorative hardware—all are easily repaired, reshaped, rebuilt or soldered (when cleaned of any protective lacquer).

Copper

Copper weighs 556 lbs. per cubic foot. It is strong, corrosion-resistant and malleable. In sheet form it can be hammered into many different shapes. Bars are often used as electrical buses. Wire can be used to form many fanciful properties. Copper can be brazed or soldered with ease. Often it is useful in arc welding as a back-up plate for aluminum or steel—to prevent the arc from burning through the work that is being welded.

The largest scenic use of copper is tubing. Copper tubing and pipe exist in sizes ranging from ⅛″ up to 8″ and larger. The smaller sizes are available in soft (easily bent) or hard straight tempers. With soft copper tubing, the most intricate decorative elements can be easily crafted with little effort other than cutting, bending and soldering this workable material. When finished, it can be stiffened by filling the bent tubing with low-melting-point Cerrobend or Hydrocal plaster. A wide line of plumbing fittings and hardware are made which can be adapted to theatrical use. Fountains and liquid effects can be made quickly and sturdily using standard plumbing techniques. The tubing is fairly expensive, but the time saved in its use, plus the resultant strength, reliability and reusability, more than justifies the cost.

Aluminum

Aluminum, once the exotic metal of the 1800s, has developed into one of the most useful theatrical metals of our time. The metal and its alloys have the general characteristic of strength with the amazingly light weight of 165 lbs. per cubic foot. In its untempered and half-tempered varieties, aluminum is easily drilled, tapped, sawed, planed and filed with hand tools from the carpenter shop. Machine operations are easily performed on these and harder alloys. Most aluminum alloys are easily bent and shaped. Conventional joining techniques—screwing, bolting and riveting—are easily accomplished in the average scene shop. However, aluminum is difficult to solder, and the average welder finds it requires much experimentation and practice to successfully weld the metal without such specialized equipment as the TIG or MIG.

It is unfortunate that many scene shops cannot afford to use aluminum or purchase the equipment to weld it, for with its strength/weight characteristics it could be the ideal theatrical metal.

One of the great advantages of aluminum is that it is readily available in bar, sheet, tubes, rounds and a variety of punched screens at most do-it-yourself stores. Metal supply houses maintain a wide stock of various sizes and thicknesses of plate and structural forms, plus a large variety of extruded structural and ornamental shapes. Commercially these are used for truck bodies, building hardware and structural units. Ice shows travel with aluminum-truss grids. Since the aluminum catalogues rarely get to the scene design rooms, lack of awareness limits the use of this metal both in the technical and design departments. It is worth investigating.

Steel

Steel is the most-used metal in theatre. Walk into a theatre: a steel grid is overhead, steel tracks guide the steel arbors for steel battens. Steel hardware abounds at every turn. It even appears in scenery from time to time.

Steel is strong, and for a metal of its characteristics, the weight of 489 lbs. per cubic foot is moderate. There are literally hundreds of steel alloys which come in a huge range of finishes, sizes and shapes. The present price for a pound of steel is about $.35, which places it well within the budget of most theatres when you consider that one pound of steel is equal to three feet of foot iron. Steel is readily available from numerous steel warehouses and jobbers around the country. Most theatres are close to some source of supply, even if it is only the ubiquitous scrap yard.

Although steel requires a different technology for its use than the usual scenic materials, with the proper tools it is relatively simple to use. It is easily drilled, tapped, filed and shaped. Steel does not need fasteners to be joined or fabricated. Although screws, rivets and bolts can be used, steel can be fused permanently into one uniform piece by welding.

There are other advantages to steel. Due to its strength, many designs can be executed easily that would be weak, difficult or impossible with other materials. Stage hardware can be fabricated to fulfill certain specialized functions. Stage equipment may be developed utilizing it. Platform systems may be designed and built simply and permanently by steel construction.

3

Steel and Aluminum Basic Alloys and Shapes

Steel

Steel is a combination of carbon and iron that is malleable to some degree. This malleability—the ability to be bent or pounded to a desired shape without failure—makes steel superior to the comparatively brittle cast iron. Variations in the amount of carbon and additions of other alloying elements make possible the manufacture of thousands of specialized steels. For theatrical purposes we need to consider only a few.

Mild Steel

Mild steel, or more properly AISI (American Iron and Steel Institute) C-1020, is the most useful general-purpose steel for theatre usage. Since it is classified as a carbon steel, there is no minimum content of any element added to obtain a desired alloying effect. In other words, this steel approaches the norm of being "plain old steel" with no properties of fantastic strength, corrosion resistance or great hardness (which are not required in most theatre applications).

AISI C-1020 is manufactured in two primary forms—*structural,* steel of reasonably uniform chemical composition, complete internal soundness

and no significant surface defects; and the common *merchant bar* variety for non-critical uses requiring mild cold bending and hot forming, punching and welding. Merchant bar steel may have surface defects and minor internal flaws.

One would use structural AISI C-1020, often listed as A-36, for permanent applications (such as a rigging system). Merchant bar-quality steel, often catalogued as AISI M-1020, would be used for scenic applications (railings, decorative grills and other non-permanent items). These are general guidelines: A-36 can be used for scenery, and M-1020 can be used in permanent construction if its strength limitations are observed.

AISI C-1020, in both forms, is a general-purpose theatrical steel which can be either hot- or cold-worked, cut and welded with ease, and which will retain an adequate amount of strength. M-1020 has a tensile strength of approximately 60,000 p.s.i. (pounds per square inch) and A-36, approximately 79,000 p.s.i.

AISI C-1018

AISI C-1018 is an open-hearth, low-carbon, general-purpose machinery steel with a medium manganese content (0.6% to 1%). It has good casehardening properties (the ability to obtain a tough, hard

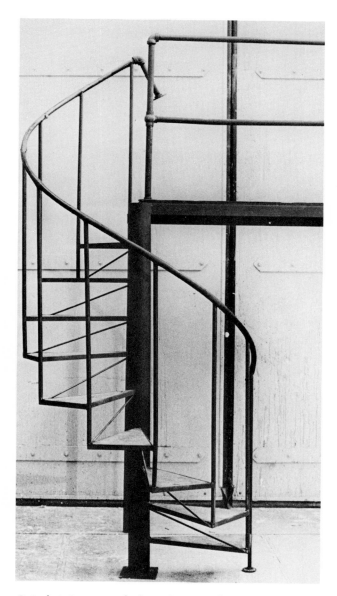

Spiral staircase made from A-36 steel.

skin over a malleable core of metal), and for old-fashioned but effective blacksmith hammer-forging, it is superb. It can be easily cold-worked, although C-1020 is better. AISI C-1018 is suitable for machine tool working due to its manganese content. It can be used for items that require machined parts with good wear resistance and that need to be welded. Machined turntable centers and axles for a variety of wheels are examples.

AISI C-1045

AISI C-1045 is a high-carbon machinery steel that may be flame-hardened. It is used for gears, shafts and high-strength bolts.

AISI A-15 & A-350

A-15 and A-350 are medium-strength carbon steels found in deformed reinforcing bars. Due to their unusual surface texture, designed to be gripped by poured concrete but aesthetically pleasing in certain types of stage design, they see limited application in scenery and properties. They can be easily bent and shaped. Welding does not produce exceptionally strong joints without special kinds of filler rod or electrodes but it is strong enough for decorative stage use with regular techniques.

These steels just listed, AISI 1020 (A-36 & M-1020), 1018, 1045, A-15 and A-350 will fill most theatrical needs. If special needs develop, consult your steel supplier—he can be most helpful.

Steel Alloy Selection Aids

The following "rules of thumb" are helpful in understanding steel alloys.
  1. The more carbon—the more strength, the greater hardness; the poorer cold-working and welding.

2. The more manganese—the more strength, the greater hardness; the poorer cold-working and welding.
3. Nickel—adds toughness and corrosion resistance.
4. Chromium—adds surface hardness, toughness and corrosion resistance.
5. Copper—adds strength without affecting welding or cold-working.
6. Lead—adds machinability to steel without reducing strength.

Ordering Steel

When ordering steel, tell the supplier the shape, size, alloy and finish for each separate item. Avoid cutting charges when possible by ordering standard lengths, usually 20′.

Steel Surfaces

Steel is available from the mill in a number of finishes.

Plain Oxide   The most common and inexpensive is the plain finish. This steel is coated with a gray oxide, usually has some degree of scale and depending upon the source of supply, varying amounts of rust. For many metalworking operations this oxide coating must be wire-brushed or ground off, particularly to insure good brazing since it interferes with the flow and alloying of the molten brass, and for painting since the oxide is an unstable base for paint on a long-term basis.

Oiled and Pickled Finish   When a clean steel surface is desired, one orders steel with the "oiled and pickled" finish. This is obtained by cleaning the hot steel in an acid bath at the mill. The acid-cleaned steel is neutralized and is then oil-coated to prevent new rust and oxide from forming. The user removes the oil with a solvent and then applies his own finish. Oiled and pickled finishes are most often found on sheet steels and tubing.

Chandelier made from reinforcing bar.

Painted and Plated Sheet steel is now available from the mill in a variety of painted finishes and colors. Steel is also available in a variety of plated finishes. This protective metallic plating is either applied from a solution by electrolysis, or is just melted into the hot metal. Copper-plated steel is done electrolytically, and galvanized steel is done by dipping. Little plating is used in theatre due to its cost, but for a brilliant metallic effect it is well worth it. Paint can never approach the brilliance of plating. Beware of galvanized coatings; they produce noxious fumes when welded or flamecut.

Aluminum

Aluminum is the second most used metal in industry. Although it is considerably more expensive on a per lb. basis, approximately $1.34 to $1.64, it has about three times the volume of steel. This means that in many situations much lighter structures of aluminum are actually stronger than those of steel. For theatre use, particularly touring shows with elaborate structures, stock turntables and the like, this factor of light weight with strength is extremely important.

Aluminum Alloys

#6061 & #6063 Like steel, aluminum may be purchased in a variety of chemical compositions or alloys. Practically speaking, #6061 and #6063 will be the alloys that the technician will rely upon for most major scenic and mechanical work. The do-it-yourself varieties will suffice for most property department requirements.

#6061 is a medium-strength aluminum alloy that has been extruded (the process of pushing metal through a die to give it a specific cross section) into many structural shapes. It is very useful for

platform and stage machinery applications. #6061, depending on its temper or degree of hardness, has a tensile strength of between 35,000 and 45,000 p.s.i. It is generally available from suppliers.

#6063 is an aluminum alloy that is superior for extrusion. Many elaborate shapes are available. In the common T-5 and T-6 tempers, #6063 has a tensile strength between 32,000 and 36,000 p.s.i. Because many truck trailers are made from this alloy, it is readily available.

#1100 #1100 is an aluminum alloy that is easy to form, readily welded, but in unworked form has little strength. This is not a disadvantage, for #1100 is particularly well suited to shaping by spinning (it gains considerable strength). It is available in sheet and plate form. (Sheet is less than ½″ thick, plate is anything thicker.)

EC EC is pure, unalloyed aluminum. It is easy to work, bend, shape, fasten and is very ductile. It is used in many extrusions. Unworked EC has a strength of 13,000 p.s.i., but when worked it may actually double its strength.

Aluminum Surfaces

While most aluminum has the standard mill finish (which may not be entirely free from stains and oil residue), other finishes are available for special projects. One side of sheet aluminum may be bright and unblemished to varying degrees and heat treatment stains may be held to the minimum. The uniform mill finish has a matte surface with no stains. Other surface finishes can be applied by the user after suitable cleaning and surface preparation. Aluminum is also available in a variety of pre-painted, plated and anodized surfaces. These range from aluminum house siding to Alzak lighting reflectors.

The preceding alloys of steel and aluminum will solve most of your metalworking requirements. If confronted with a problem that these alloys will not solve, consult the various steel and aluminum handbooks and check with the suppliers. Somewhere out there is an alloy that will be just the right solution to your problem.

Commercial Forms and Processes of Steel and Aluminum

Casting

There are several processes by which various steel and aluminum shapes are made. The first is casting (molten metal is poured into a mold for the desired object, is allowed to cool and solidify and the mold is removed). While it is possible to do limited aluminum casting in a well-equipped shop, most technicians rely on the commercial foundry for their steel and aluminum casting needs. Wooden patterns with the proper shrink allowances for the particular metal are prepared for the desired object, the foundry casts the item in sand or plaster molds and the customer does any required finishing.

Many standard items of stage equipment are cast from steel. Counterweight bricks and lighting boom bases are two examples.

A note about die casting aluminum. It requires complicated molds and elaborate casting machinery, but die cast aluminum is used in many hardware and machine parts. Most power handtools use many die castings, and one major line of lighting equipment features extensive use of die cast aluminum in its instruments.

Forging

Forging is the process by which hot aluminum or steel is pounded with or into a die to form the desired shape. This pounding alters the arrangement of the metal's grain structure from a crystalline to a more linear form which increases its strength (since the grain structure follows the shape of the forged object). Since the cost of the dies is great, the theatre is limited to commercial items, unless one is willing to hand-forge steel like the old-time blacksmith did. Commercially, forgings are found in stage screws, bolts and other hardware.

Rolling

Most of the steel that is used by the technician is rolled. Usually the more ductile alloys of steel (AISI 1020 or 1018) may be obtained in cold rolled sheet and bar, at least in the smaller sizes and shapes. This cold forming is beneficial to the steel's internal structure, in a manner similiar to forging, and increases its tensile strength to a significant degree. Note that the lower carbon and manganese content of cold rolled shapes allows easy welding.

Hot rolled steel shapes are either those sizes of the low-carbon steels which are too large for economical cold rolling, or the high-carbon manganese steels which are not ductile enough to be successfully cold rolled. Hot rolled steel shapes are generally cheaper than cold rolled.

Aluminum ingots are usually reduced to sheet form by rolling. The ingot is heated and rolled from thicknesses of up to 25″ down to an intermediate thickness of approximately 1″. The hot rolled plate may then be cold rolled to the desired sheet thickness, a process in which it gains considerable cold-worked strength.

Sheet, rod and bar are the usual rolled aluminum products. Special shapes may be rolled in a number of intermediate steps.

21

Extruding

Most aluminum shapes that are useful in the theatre are extruded, a process practically unique to aluminum. In its simplest form, extrusion is the technique of pushing an ingot of aluminum through a steel die that squeezes it to the desired cross section. Since this is a hot process—the aluminum is heated to reduce its strength and help it flow in the extrusion process, and the friction of the die adds considerable heat—all aluminum extrusions that will need great strength must be heat-treatable alloys since there is no cold-worked strength gained in this process.

While the extrusion process is impossible for the scene shop to do, it is possible to have dies made and aluminum extruded for a particular shape. Extrusions may have elaborate cross sections and much fabricating time may be saved by using a specialized extrusion instead of building up a shape from numerous parts or machining it down from solid stock. However, the cost of this is high in terms of most theatre budgets, so any custom extrusions you might have done should have a commercial market.

Drawing

Drawing is similar to extruding, but the steel or aluminum is pulled through the die instead of being pushed. Wire, tubing and rod are typical products.

4

Steel and Aluminum Shapes and Uses

Steel and aluminum are sold in a variety of shapes in various alloys. Here are some of the more common ones available:

Channels

The channel is a shape with a wide central plate or web and two smaller plates or flanges at right angles on edge. Channels are rolled in several cross sectional thicknesses.

Steel Ship and Car Channel

The ship and car channel is characterized by a very thick web which makes it the strongest of the channels. These are usually hot rolled from A-36 steel. Ship and car channels are available in web widths from 3″ to 10″ at one-inch intervals and in larger sizes at two-inch intervals. These channels are made only as small as the 3″ web; because their strength is usually in excess of the required strength of scenery, there is little call for this type. Exceptions are for major, heavy-duty structural work, such as headblock beams.

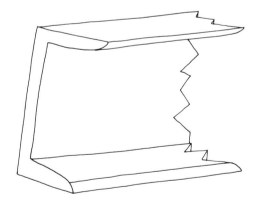

Channel cross section.

Steel Structural Channel

Structural channel is made from A-36 steel in the same sizes as ship and car channel, but with a thinner cross section. Although this type is not produced in a size under 3″, there are many possible uses for it in long, open platform spans, pageant wagon frames, etc. Steel structural channel is approximately two-thirds the weight and strength of ship and car channel. For modest theatre loadings it is more than adequate.

Aluminum Structural Channel

Structural channel is also made from aluminum. It is extruded from Alloy #2061 with a T-6 temper and is commonly available in widths from 3″ to 12″. These channels have the standard tapering flanges as do the steel ones. 3″ channel weighs about 1.7 lbs. per foot; 12″ channel weighs about 9 lbs. per foot. Since steel weighs approximately three times as much as an equal volume of aluminum, it would be possible to use a much larger channel of aluminum that would have greater structural efficiency than the same weight of steel.

Steel Junior Channel

Steel junior channel is characterized by a very small web thickness in proportion to its size. Strength results from shape, not from the mass of steel. Unfortunately, they are available in only 10″ and 12″ sizes. Commercially these are used as lightweight stair stringers. Perhaps they could be used for long-span platforms, etc.

Steel Bar Size Channel

Steel bar size channel is made from hot rolled AISI 1020 steel of merchant bar quality. These channels are made in 19 sizes from ¾″ to 2½″ widths. Webs vary from 5/16″ to 5/8″ and in thickness from 1/8″ to ¼″. These are small enough to be useful in steel-framed scenery, special platforms and show machinery.

Aluminum Special Channels

Recently new designs of aluminum channel have been extruded. These are designed to use the structural abilities of aluminum to full advantage instead of using a shape that was designed for the most efficient use of steel. These channels use parallel surfaces in their flanges which greatly aid in structural fabrication. Other channels have a flange added to their flange, making a hat-shaped cross section. These are designed to stiffen sheet aluminum, as in truck trailer construction. Some of the channels have rounded corners, others have sharp edges. There are 20 new channel shapes (see Appendix A). These channels should allow interesting possibilities in structural scenery.

Uses for Channels

Channels should be used where the main stress is against the main web axis and where secondary forces are stressing from the smooth side of the main web toward the flanges. Channels should be used where they can be adequately braced to prevent lateral buckling or when they are used in joined pairs back-to-back (as in a pair of steel-framed stairs). Channels should not be used when the main stress is perpendicular to the flanges for structural economy; they are not designed for that form of stress, and failure may result.

I Beams

Steel I Beams

There are two main types of I beams: the wide flange beam (sometimes confused with the H column which has a shorter web) and the simple I beam. The wide flange beam will resist forces from either axis; the I beam is designed to resist stress applied to its long axis. Both are usually rolled from A-36 or high-strength steel. Since the smallest size for a steel I beam is 3″, it is limited in its use on stage. However for special, permanent projects I beams are indispensable.

Steel Junior I Beams

Steel junior I beams have thin cross sections and rely on shape instead of mass for strength. Their light weight is an advantage in stage use, and they have adequate strength for typical loadings. These are made in 6″, 8″, 10″ and 12″ sizes which are, unfortunately, rather large for most things other than permanent equipment or massive scenery.

Aluminum I Beams

Aluminum is extruded in a variety of I beam shapes, usually from #6061 or #6063 alloy with a T-6 temper. Standard I beams that have a similar shape to steel I's are available in sizes from 3″ to 12″. Weights vary from about 2 lbs. per foot for the 3″ I to about 11 lbs. per foot for the 12″. A very small H beam is extruded that has a web 4″ tall and flanges 4″ wide. Special I beams with parallel sides to their flanges are obtainable in 6″ to 12″ sizes. Special H beams are made with webs 1½″ or 2″ tall and flanges 2″ wide. These could have scenic use since they combine strength with small sizes and weights of about ¾ lb. per foot.

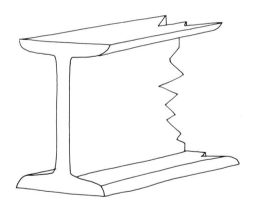

I beam cross section.

25

Uses For I Beams

Steel and aluminum I beams are used in situations where the primary stress is parallel to the web. The flanges on both ends of the web add considerable bracing against lateral bending and allow the beam to be used with less bracing than the channel with its one-sided web.

Angles

Steel Angles

Angles are, by far, one of the most used steel shapes. They can be used to stiffen scenery or to build hundreds of stage structures and scenic units.

Steel Bar-Sized Angles

Bar-sized angles are rolled from AISI 1020 merchant bar steel in 48 sizes ranging from ½″ x ½″ x ⅛″ to 2½″ x 2½″ x ½″. These are small enough to be of great use in scenic construction as well as in stage machinery and equipment. Standard length is 20′.

Steel Structural Angles

Steel structural angles are available in sizes from 3″ x 2″ x ³⁄₁₆″ up to 8″ x 8″ x ½″ in 98 sizes. These are useful if you have aesthetic or loading requirements that demand larger sizes, or if you are making an assembly in which an angle might replace two pieces of plate welded together at 90°. Remember, steel angles come with unequal sides, as well as equal.

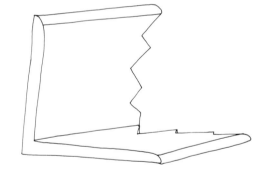

Angle cross section.

Aluminum Angles

Aluminum is extruded in a variety of angle shapes, usually from #6061 or #6063 alloy with a T-6 temper. There are approximately 48 sizes of standard angle with equal legs. These range in size from ¾″ x ¾″ x ⅛″ up to 8″ x 8″ x 1″. Standard length is 25′. This shape approximates that of the standard steel angle. Unequal leg angle is made in 64 sizes, varying from 1¼″ x ¾″ x ³/₃₂″ up to 8″ x 6″ x ¾″. Again, the cross sections of these angles resemble those of steel. Special aluminum angles are extruded with parallel sides to their legs. The edges may be either sharp or rounded on the inside edge, and the legs may be equal or unequal. There are 54 sizes which range from ½″ x ½″ x ¹/₁₆″ up to 5¼″ x 2¼″ x ⅛″. (See Appendix A.)

Uses for Angles

Angles are used where there should be resistance to vertical and horizontal stress along the main axis. Although there is a tendency for the angle to buckle by twisting or having the two legs collapse, this is prevented by other angles resisting in the opposite direction in a well-designed structure. Wagon tracks and rails, platform framing and stair treads are typical uses. Aluminum angles are frequently applied to the edges of road boxes, speaker cabinets and counters to give protection and aesthetic trim.

Bars

Steel Bars

Steel bars (square or rectangular solid stock) are available in a number of types of steel, either hot or cold rolled, and in a huge number of sizes. AISI merchant bar and 1018 are the most common steels used.

Aluminum Bars

Aluminum bars are generally available in 12′ or 16′ lengths of #6061 or #6063 alloy with a T-5 to T-6 temper. These are extruded with sharp corners and are either square or rectangular in cross section. Sizes range from ¼″ square to 4″ square, and from ⅛″ x ½″ to 3″ x 6″ rectangular. (See Appendix A.) The smaller sizes are usually used in scenery and machinery as they are, but the larger ones are the raw material for machined parts.

Uses for Bars

Bars are a basic shape that can be used in many structures. They should be used so that the primary stress is parallel to their longest axis. Often bars are welded together to make special angle stock. Various braces and corner irons are often bent or welded from bar stock. They are used in decorative grillwork since their shape allows for easy bending along their thinner axis.

Plate and Sheet

Steel Plate and Sheet

Most steel plate and sheet is rolled from A-36 steel. Plate is considered to be anything over ¾″ thick—rather heavy for theatrical uses. Steel has its thickness listed in gauge numbers, which differ approximately 0.5 per number. U.S. standard numbers are used. They are listed in Appendix B.

Aluminum Plate and Sheet

Aluminum plate (anything thicker than ¼″) and sheet (anything thinner) are rolled in a wide selection of alloys and tempers. For theatre use, one would probably specify flat rather than coiled sheet of #6061 or #6063 alloy with a T-5 or T-6 temper. Thickness is given in thousandths of an inch and sheet sizes vary from 36″ to 72″ wide, from 96″ to 144″ long (although it is possible to obtain much larger sizes intended for trailer roofing). Other specialty sheets are available. Plate is readily available in thicknesses from .250″ to 1.0″, widths from 24″ to 72″ and lengths from 72″ to 144″. Mention should be made of aluminum foil—any sheet that is less than 0.006″ thick.

Uses for Plate and Sheet

Plate and sheet are to metal what plywood is to wood. They may be used as a high-strength, heat-resistant covering material or as sources for parts and pieces. Remember that various finishes and embossed textures are available on sheet metal. The various roofing and siding materials, ranging from the old standby, corrugated iron, to the new aluminum ribbed and vee industrial sidings and aluminum house siding, could add that special touch and practicality to many realistic settings. There are many possibilities.

Tee cross section.

Tees

Steel Tees—Bar-sized

Steel bar-size tees are hot rolled from AISI M-1020 steel. Sizes range from flange width of ¾″, stem height of ¾″ and thickness of ⅛″ to 2½″ x 2½″ x ⅜″. These are quite suitable for lighter duty.

Steel Structural Tees

Structural tees are hot rolled from A-36 steel. Their sizes range from 3″ x 2½″ x $^5/_{16}$″ to 5″ x 3⅛″ x ½″ in 7 sizes. These are for heavy-duty use.

Aluminum Tees

Aluminum tees are extruded from #6061 or #6063 alloy with a T-5 and T-6 temper. There are 5 cross sectional types (See Appendix A.) Sizes range from ¾″ x ¾″ x ⅛″ to 2″ x 2″ x ¼″.

Uses for Tees

Tees are used where the stress is not strong enough to justify an I beam. They resist vertical and horizontal stresses without the collapsing and rotational characteristics of angles. In standard fastening techniques, tees may be easily fastened on both sides of their stems, a strength-giving, stiffening feature. Tees are used for structures that require thin but long sections, such as portal legs. They are used for structural stiffening and framing and are often used to support hung acoustical ceilings.

Rods

Steel Rod

Rods are available in a variety of carbon steels and finishes. Sizes are available from ⅛″ to 10″ varying by 1/16″ diameters in the smaller sizes. For standard scenic or construction use, the hot rolled steel round of AISI M-1020 may be used for tension members or as decorative metal work. For more demanding use, as in stage equipment, the C-1018 cold-finished steel round is useful. This may be hardened and used for shafting or axles. Remember the concrete deformed reinforcing rods for decorative work; they are cheap and workable.

Aluminum Rod

In aluminum, any size with a diameter of ⅜″ or more is rod; less than ⅜″ it is wire. Rod is extruded in #6061 or #6063 with tempers from T-5 to T-6. It comes in 12′ lengths up to a diameter of 2¾″. Larger diameters are available in shorter lengths up to 8″. (See Appendix A.) Diameters are standard.

Aluminum Trim

Aluminum is extruded in a variety of trim shapes; some of these could have decorative use on the stage. (See Appendix A.)

Pipe

Steel Pipe

Steel pipe is made from an alloy that has a compression-tensile strength of 36,000 p.s.i. It is available in three wall thicknesses and strengths: standard weight, extra strong and double-extra strong. The pipe size given is the internal diameter of standard weight pipe. This decreases for the two heavier sizes. For example, a 1″ pipe would have a wall thickness of 0.133″, 0.179″ and 0.358″ respectively. The outside diameter would remain 1.315″ for all three weights.

Twenty-foot is the standard pipe length. Usually the ends of each piece come threaded for fittings, but recently this practice seems to be waning. For welding this is an improvement; for standard pipe fitting, you have that much more threading to do.

Aluminum Pipe

Aluminum pipe is sold in 20′ lengths in the same diameters as steel. However, its wall thickness is different. 1½″ standard aluminum pipe has a wall thickness of .145″ and a weight of .940 lbs. per foot. Featherweight pipe of the same diameter is .065 thick and weighs only .441 lbs. per foot. Light pipe (not related to stage electricity) is .109″ thick and weighs .721 lbs. per foot; extra heavy 1½″ diameter pipe has a .200″ wall and weighs 1.256 lbs. per foot. The alloys of pipe are usually #6061-T6 or #6063T-6 and occasionally #3003-H14.

Sizes of Pipe

Pipe is commonly available in diameters of ⅛″ to 3″ in steel. Sizes from 4″ to 12″ can be ordered. Extra strong and double-extra strong steel pipe is available in ½″ diameters upward. Aluminum pipe is commonly available in most sizes at aluminum supply companies, not from plumbing wholesalers.

Uses for Pipe

Pipe will resist a moderate stress from any direction better than any other shape of equivalent mass. It may be used for structure (particularly as columns), decorative use and railing. Since steel pipe in particular is widely used in the plumbing industry, it is the most available steel shape. A note of caution: steel pipe is the best material for counterweight and hemp battens; aluminum tends to bend too much under uneven loadings in this service.

Tubing

Steel Tubing, Square and Rectangular

Although there is no hard distinction between pipe and tubing, a general rule is that pipe is sold by its internal diameter (based on its regular wall thickness) and tubing is sold by its external diameter or overall size.

There are many kinds of steel tubing. It is generally square, rectangular or round in cross section although hexagonal, oval and streamline (teardrop shaped) are available in limited sizes. Structural square tubing is sold in the following sizes:

12″ x 12″, 10″ x 10″ & 8′ x 8″ with thicknesses from ½″ to ¼″

7″ x 7″, 6″ x 6″ & 5″ x 5″ with thicknesses from ½″ to ³⁄₁₆″

4″ x 4″ with thicknesses from ⅜″ to ³⁄₁₆″

3½″ x 3½″ and 3″ x 3″ with thicknesses from ⁵⁄₁₆″ to ³⁄₁₆″

Rectangular structural tubing is sold in the following sizes: 12″ x 6″, 10″ x 6″, 8″ x 6″, 8″ x 4″, 8″ x 3″, 7″ x 5″, 6″ x 4″, 6″ x 3″, 6″ x 2″, 5″ x 3″, 5″ x 2″, 4″ x 3″, 4″ x 2″ and 3″ x 2″ in the same range of thickness as the square variety.

Regular steel tubing is made in square cross sections in sizes from:

⅜″ x ⅜″ to 1¼″ x 1¼″ in ⅛″ intervals in thicknesses from .035 to .065″.

1½″ x 1½″ to 2½″ x 2½″ in ¼″ intervals in thicknesses from .065 to ⅛″ typical.

3″ x 3″ is made in thicknesses up to ½″.

Steel Tubing, Round

Round steel tubing is manufactured in the following sizes:

⅛″ to 2″ diameters in ¹⁄₁₆″ intervals

2″ to 7¾″ diameters in ⅛″ intervals

Larger sizes are available up to 16″ in diameter.

Typical thicknesses for steel tubing are:

⅛″ with a wall thickness of .020″ to .035″

½″ with a wall thickness of .016″ to .188″

1″ with a wall thickness of .028″ to .375″

2″ with a wall thickness of .028″ to .750″

4″ with a wall thickness of .049″ to 1.250″

6″ with a wall thickness of .065″ to 2.000″

There are many other specialized steel tubings for specific applications—from roll bars on race cars to cylinders of hydraulic systems. If confronted with a problem that regular steel tubing might not handle, consult your steel distributor; he might be able to solve the problem.

Steel Conduit

One of the most common steel tubing systems is electrical conduit. This is sold in two forms: rigid (or

Set built with round steel tubing, construction detail.

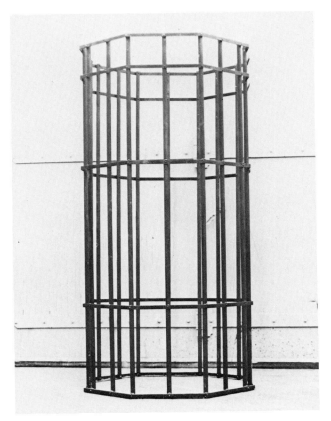

Cage made from bar stock and conduit.

Hand winch made with Unistrut.

heavy wall) and E.M.T. (electrical metallic tubing or thin wall). Rigid is sold in nominal internal diameters of ½″, ¾″, 1″, 1¼″, 1½″, 2″, 2½″, 3″, 3½″, 4″, 5″ and 6″. E.M.T. has ⅜″, ½″, ¾″, 1″, 1¼″, 1½″ and 2″ sizes. Thin wall can be bent with simple conduit benders or hickeys. Both thicknesses, however, are galvanized, which causes noxious fumes to be released during brazing or welding.

Aluminum Tubing

Aluminum tubing is drawn in round cross section from #3003-H14 and #6061-T-6 in 12′ lengths. Diameters start at ³/₁₆″ with thicknesses from .022″ to .049″ and go to 1⅛″ diameter that is between .035″ and .065″ thick. Above this diameter the tube may be extruded up to a 3″ diameter and up to .250″ thick.

Structural round aluminum tube is extruded in diameters from 1½″ to 6″ with thicknesses generally .188″ to .250″. Alloys #6061 or #6063 with a T-6 temper are standard.

Square and rectangular tubes are extruded in #6063-T-5 in 21′ 1″ lengths. Square tubes range from ¾″ x ¾″ x .062″ thick up to 4″ x 4″ x .188″. Rectangular tubes start at ½″ x 1″ x .125″ and go to 3″ x 6″ x .188″. (See Appendix A.)

Uses for Tubing

Round tubing may be used like pipe for lightweight structures; railing, furniture, jail bars and the like. Seamless tubing is available in telescoping sizes. Curves can be bent relatively easily with simple equipment. Square and rectangular tubing are particularly useful for replacing the wooden 1″ x 1″ railings, window frames and any lightly framed structure that actors run into as well as for flat framing and platform structure. Tubing can be fastened by a variety of commercial fasteners, brazed or welded. Steel tubing welds especially well with the MIG unit. Tubing is one of the most useful group of shapes for theatrical use.

Proprietary Shapes

Several companies make special shapes, usually from steel, that make up a variety of structural systems. Several are quite useful.

Unistrut

Unistrut is probably the most used proprietary shape in theatre. It is produced by the Unistrut Company, Wayne, Michigan 48184. This system uses a group of U-shaped channels that bolt together with special spring-loaded nuts and joining brackets. Many scenic and stage equipment items may be made with this material: theatre buildings (literally!), lighting grids, stairways, racks, platforms. Think of it as a giant erector set. The advantage of the material is that it only takes simple cutting and bolting to use. The disadvantage is that it requires a lot of relatively expensive fittings and the final result might look a little too industrial for some design situations.

Telespar

Unistrut makes a system of telescoping square steel tubes that is known as Telespar. Tubes are available in sizes from 1½″ x 1½″ up to 2½″ x 2½″ with ⅜″ holes on all 4 sides punched every 1″ on center. Plain tubes are available in telescoping sizes from 1″ x 1″ to 2½″ x 2½″. Telespar is available in a plain or galvanized finish. This is a nice material for theatrical use; inventories may be built up slowly, and because of the telescoping feature, various lengths may be used without cutting. It can, however, be cut easily with a power hacksaw; it can be welded for odd-angle corners. Sets may be designed around this material, either using it as hidden structure or as a design motif in its own right.

Detail illustrating strength, Telespar set for *All's Well That Ends Well*; Carolyn Ross, designer.

Slotted Angle

Slotted angle is pressed in various sizes that have a variety of holes and slots punched into them so pieces may be bolted together without additional drilling. Special shears are sold to cut the angle to length with ease. Dexion (trademark) and Interlake make two systems using this concept. Slotted angle is a handy material for those operations that do not weld; it is also highly reusable.

Conclusion

The materials listed in this chapter should suffice in a great many theatrical situations. However, they are not all that is available. Do not be afraid to look for additional metals, shapes and products. Remember the junkyard. Theatre is eclectic—it thrives on what it can get from the non-theatrical world!

5

Metal Shaping

Metals can be shaped without loss of mass by bending, hand forging, casting, spinning and rolling. Metal can also be sawed, cut, filed and machined down to a desired size and shape. Here are some techniques applicable to theatre.

Metal Bending

Most metals can be bent. Thinner stock, like sheet, is bent cold; thicker metals are softened by heat and then bent hot. Heat may be used when the metal is so brittle that it would crack when bent cold. Heating steel to a red heat by a torch, forge or even a charcoal grill allows sharp bends to be made easily. Slow cooling allows the heated metal to return to its original characteristics unless it has been tempered or heat treated. In that case the tempering or heat treating must be redone.

Bending Calculations

A bend uses up some of the metal's length. As a rule, when bending soft steel, brass and aluminum, add ⅓ of the stock's thickness to the total length of the material for each bend. If hard metals are used, add ½ of their thickness instead of ⅓.

If total accuracy is required, one of these formulas from *Machinery's Handbook* should be applied:

L equals length in inches of straight stock required before bending.

T equals thickness in inches.

R equals inside radius of bend in inches.

For 90° bends in half-hard copper and brass, soft steel and aluminum:
L equals (0.64 x T) plus (1.57 x R) plus sum of straight sides.

For 90° bends in soft brass and soft copper:
L equals (0.55 x T) plus (1.57 x R) plus sum of the straight lengths.

For 90° bends in bronze, hard copper, cold rolled steel and spring steel:
L equals (0.71 x T) plus (1.57 x R) plus sum of the straight lengths.

For angles other than 90°, find length L using the above formulas, multiply L by the angle of the bend in degrees divided by 90. This will give you the length of the stock required. Remember that metal must often be bent beyond the desired angle because it will tend to spring back. Trial and error determines the amount of necessary overbend.

35

How to Bend Metal with Little or No Equipment

Metal shapes may be bent using simple equipment. Heat aids the process, particularly with steel. The metal is heated to red hot and is then easily bent. The area of heating will help determine the radius of the bend, i.e., a small hot area will bend sharper than a larger, cooler one. Often additional leverage is helpful: place the stock, either hot or cold, between heavy pipe railings, columns or even between the sections of an old radiator (not the one providing the shop's heat). This will give the needed fulcrum for a bend or series of bends. A piece of pipe slipped over the end of the stock will give the additional leverage needed to bend all the way to the end. Long, large radius bends are done by taking a series of short, shallow bends. While crude, this process will work for rod, pipe and bar stock, but angles and other shapes tend to crimp.

Bending Patterns and Layout

It is helpful when bending large curves and irregular shapes to lay out the plan on the shop floor. Grid the floor with a chalkline to match the drafting and chalk out the plan. If several identical lengths are to be bent, it is helpful to paint the pattern on the floor with scrap scene paint. Paper patterns have a way of catching fire and while plywood patterns and templates are useful, they do char.

Simple Bending Equipment

A few pieces of simple equipment will facilitate bending. A vise, 5″ or larger, will allow you to clamp the stock and get sharper bends than any freehand bending technique will allow. Simply heat the steel red hot, clamp it in the vise at the proper place (this may be marked by centerpunching or soapstone) and bend the piece while pounding down on the bend with a hammer. A good, sharp, 90° bend should result.

A blacksmith's anvil weighing at least 100 lbs. is a very versatile tool. It should be fastened to a log, end grain up, at a convenient working height. While

Anvil.

this seems a bit early American, it is the simplest way to support and cushion the anvil. Metal may be bent to a sharp angle by pounding it over the edges of the anvil's face, or curved by bending and pounding it around the horn. Cable may be cut with a cold chisel on its table (never anywhere else), and a variety of pounding forms, or stakes, may be fitted into the hardie hole for more sophisticated forging projects like raising containers (the process of pounding up the sides of a disk into cylindrical form). For decorative ironwork the anvil is indispensable.

E.M.T. conduit is best bent by using a hickey or conduit bender. Either is available in sizes to match the conduit. Simply hook the bender onto the conduit and lever it back. As the conduit bends, the sides of the bender support the walls of the material and prevent it from crimping. Relatively sharp bends are done easily with these tools.

Hickey in use.

Metal Bending Machinery—the Brake

Although much metal is simply bent on an anvil or in a vise, metal-bending machinery is particularly helpful for duplication of bends, speed and quality workmanship without much operator skill. For bending sheet metal, the brake is most useful. Basically it consists of a fixed metal bed on which the sheet is placed, a top leaf with a changeable shaping nose that clamps down on the sheet and a bending leaf that is pivoted to the front of the bed. Any sheet that protrudes beyond the bed is lifted by the bending leaf and pushed against the shaping nose to bend it. Various guides, jigs and nose piece combinations are usually available for special bends. Usually the clamping action of the top leaf is controlled by a foot treadle, the bending by a hand lever. Sheet may also be bent in a similar manner by clamping it between layers of wood, but a brake is superior.

Brake.

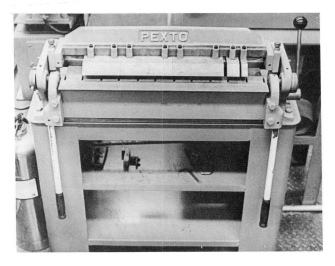

Use of the Brake To use the brake, place the sheet on the bending table, align it with the nose piece edge in the center of the arc calculated for the bend, clamp it with the top leaf and push the master lever until the bend is completed. Various sections of the nose piece may be moved or changed to adapt to special bending situations. Always consult the instructions for the brake you are using.

The Metal Roll

Often a sheet or bar must be bent to a gradual radius or circle; this is best done on the metal roll. Basically the machine consists of two fixed rollers and one adjustable roller between them. By moving the adjustable roller in, the metal is bent to a tighter radius as it is rolled through. The rollers are usually powered by a hand crank.

The Metal Bender

Most metal-bending machines bend their work with a movable die acting against two fixed dies. The dies or forming blocks are changeable. These support the metal as it bends and prevent undue deformity. Dies are available to fit angle, bar, tubing, rod and pipe, and it is possible to make dies to fit special shapes. Metal-bending machines, like the Hossfeld #2, usually have the capacity to bend sections like 2½" pipe to a radius of 6" or less.

The bender, with a complete set of dies, is a tremendously flexible machine. However, the only way to operate it is with instruction book in hand, for with so many possibilities, the chance for error increases. Follow the directions and these machines are simple to use.

Remember, cold-working of metal hardens it, often to the point where additional work will crack it. To prevent this, when you feel the metal getting hard, stop the work and anneal it. This is usually done by heating and gradual cooling for steel and aluminum; copper can be heated and quenched.

Metal Spinning

Although metal bowls, cups, goblets and similar shapes may be pounded out by hand, a quicker way to obtain (and particularly to duplicate) these items is metal spinning. For this process you need a variable-speed lathe of at least ½ hp. with good, heavy thrust bearings. A form, or chuck, is turned

Roll.

Metal bender.

Metal-spinning chuck.

Metal-spinning in progress.

Metal-spinning tools.

Partly spun disk on metal-spinning chuck.

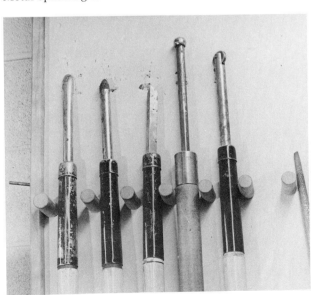

Annealing the partly spun disk.

Finishing spinning the disk.

from hardwood and is attached to the face plate. As in vacuum forming, no undercuts are allowed! A disk of metal, say .050″ thick, is clamped to the base of the chuck by a wooden follow block mounted on a live center in the tailstock. The disk is centered, locked in place with the follow block and lubricated with tallow and oil or soap. Speed will vary from about 300 r.p.m. to 1,800 r.p.m. depending on the material and the skill of the spinner. The lathe is started and a pointed spinning tool is placed against the tool-rest pin with its point against the center of the disk. Pressure is levered against the disk as the tool is pulled across the disk. The metal will begin to roll around the chuck. If the disk becomes work-hardened, stop the lathe, remove the work and anneal it. When the piece is completely formed, use a cutting tool to trim the top, file, burnish and the piece is complete. The property department should find this technique useful for shapes not available commercially.

Cutting Metal—Shearing

Sheet metal may be cut by using hand shears or tin snips. All the varieties of these depend on the action of opposed cutting edges, just like common paper scissors. However, there are a number of types of hand shears: straight-bladed snips, useful for larger straight line work; curved snips for cutting circles; universal shears, or duckbill snips, will do pretty well for most theatre applications. Remember, shears and snips are for cutting sheet metal, not cable and wire! For accurate work, cut a little out from the line desired, and finish with a file. (The line may be made more visible by using layout dye and then scribing it.)

A disadvantage of metal shears and tin snips is that they bend the edges of the material as they cut; this has been corrected by the development of portable power shears that use a short, reciprocating shearing blade against its own resisting, supporting edge. These machines can follow cutting lines with speed and accuracy. There is also the nibbler, both hand and power-operated. This works by punching out small squares of metal as it moves down a line. It can be used to shape holes and internal square corners without distortion of the metal.

The Shear

The metal shear is a major piece of metal shop equipment that cuts with a heavy blade sliding against a resisting, supporting edge, much like a paper cutter. The sheet metal to be cut is clamped with the cutting line on the edge, the blade is lowered with the foot treadle and the metal is cleanly cut in a straight line. Usually the shear comes equipped with various clamping and guiding jigs. Observe the thickness limitations of your shear.

Shearing is the fastest, most accurate method of straight-cutting sheet metal. It should be considered a necessary technique if much sheet metal work is to be done in your theatre shop.

Metal Saws and Sawing

Most metal-cutting saws use the principle of a sharpened tooth scraping material from a cut. Some sheet-metal saws are based on a toothless disk that relies on high speed to generate enough friction to melt its way through the sheet. Abrasive disks that are used like saws are common.

Types of Metal Saws

Metal-cutting saws are made in three main types: reciprocating, as in the hand hacksaw, sabre saw and power hacksaw; the band saw in portable and permanent versions; and circular, which may be mounted in a table, swing, radial or portable saw frame.

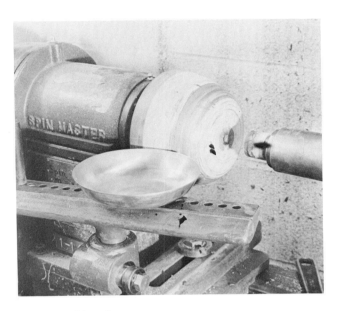

Completed bowl.

Shear.

Hand Hacksaws and Their Use

Hand hacksaw blades are usually ½″ wide, 0.025″ thick and 10″ or 12″ long. They have 14,18, 24 or 32 teeth per inch. The larger-toothed blades are used for sawing softer metals and large shapes. Finer-toothed blades are for harder material or for sawing very thin stock. A good rule of thumb is to keep three teeth on the work at all times; this will make the cut go easier and prolong blade life. An 18- or 24-tooth blade is adequate for most scene shop work.

To cut with a hacksaw, use a long, steady stroke. Apply pressure on the forward stroke and raise the blade slightly on the return. (The blade is clamped in the hacksaw frame with the teeth pointing away from you.) Don't bear down too hard—the blade will wander. It helps to have the work firmly clamped in a vise. Round stock may be held securely by the use of a vee block. Several pieces of metal may be sawed simultaneously if all are held securely.

Sabre Saws

The woodworking sabre saw may be used for metal cutting when fitted with the appropriate blade. **Safety glasses are a must** because most of the machines run at a speed fast enough to hurl hot metal particles into operator eye range. The saw and the work must be held firmly to prevent blade breakage. Use of a coolant (cutting oil works) will prolong blade life. Used properly, the sabre saw is an effective metalworking tool, especially useful for cutting irregular shapes from heavy sheet or plate.

The Power Hacksaw

Some forgotten genius must have tired of hand hacksawing and come up with a mechanism that duplicated the action of the human arm with the hacksaw. While these machines are slower than the cut-off band saw, they are fairly foolproof and require little tending when cutting large stock. Some

Sawing with an abrasive disk.

Power hacksaw.

are designed to shut themselves off when cutting is complete. Blades are much the same as for hand hacksaws but are usually 1″ wide in industrial versions. Avoid the very light-duty machines for scene shop work; buy a light industrial or heavy-duty machine if possible—it will outlast you if you keep it oiled. Remember to support long pieces being cut; stands the same height as the saw may be built for that purpose. Do not oil the blade.

Band Saws

Band saws are made in three main types: the hand-held portable version; the horizontal, table- or stand-mounted, cut-off type; the large, multispeed, vertical machine. All types require precise adjustment of the blade guides to cut accurately and a cutting pressure that will keep cutting but will not deflect or break the blade. The cut-off varieties have automatic feeds that can be adjusted to take care of this.

Band Saw Blades Correct blade selection is essential for proper cutting by the band saw. The blade choice depends on the material being cut, the speed of cutting and the desired finish of the cut. Useful types of blades for scenic use are:

Precision, or standard pitch, blades are used with fairly low cutting speeds on metal, wood and plastic. They are available in raker and wave sets.

Skip-tooth or buttress blades that are raker set are used for sawing thick metal, iron and steel and for fast cutting of wood, plastic and non-ferrous metal. Remember that the work should not be thin enough to get between the teeth and break them.

Claw-tooth blades have the same tooth spacing as skip-tooth blades but the teeth lean forward 10° (positive rake). This gives a free-cutting action on steel and aluminum, wood and plastic.

Metal-cutting band saw.

Band saw blades.

Straight set   Spring temper   Claw tooth

Wave set   Friction   Cut-off

Raker set   Buttress   Precision

Cut-off bands have 6 to 24 teeth per inch (pitch) and are raker set. These are used for production cutting of aluminum, steel and other metal. They would be most useful in a cut-off band saw for a scene shop since they handle most cutting needs.

Sawing has the advantage of making cuts in metal without creating stress, deflection or deformity as other processes may do. It is not as fast as shearing but it can cut odd shapes and heavier cross sections than the shear. Its finish is superior to flamecutting.

Pipe and Tubing Cutters

Pipe and tubing cutters depend on a hardened steel cutting wheel being forced into the pipe as the tool is rotated around it. They make a nice, square cut in very little time. If the pipe is going to be used for liquid or gas, the inside of the cut should be reamed to remove the ridge of metal left by the cutting wheel, as this will restrict flow. A pipe vise is useful for holding the pipe being cut.

Flamecutting

Red hot steel will burn when a stream of pure oxygen is directed on it. Oxyacetylene flamecutting uses this principle for fast, easy cutting of steel. (Refer to the oxyacetylene section on page 75.)

Files and Filing

There are three types of hand files: regular or American; Swiss or foreign; and special purpose. These categories are based on the grade of the cut. Swiss files range from the very coarse #8 down to the very fine #00. Regular files use a reverse grading system: #00 is rough, #0 is bastard, #1 is first cut, #2 is second cut or smooth and anything beyond is

Pipe cutter.

Files, single cut and double cut.

Single cut

Double cut

supersmooth. Availability will cause most scene shops to use the regular or American file system.

These files are made in two standard cuts: single, which has teeth running in one direction; and double cut, which has two sets of teeth running in opposite, diagonal directions. There are also curved teeth for soft metals and a small variety of proprietary cuts made for special purposes. Remember that the cut of the file varies with its size—a large file has coarser teeth than a small file, even though they are sold by the same grade of cut.

Machinist's Files

These are regular files that are best used for metal shaping in the theatre. They are available in lengths from 4″ to 18″; 12″ is a useful size. Shapes vary: flat, square, triangular or 3-square, round, half-round and knife. All come in bastard, second cut and smooth cut. Most are double cut for faster working.

File Selection and Use

Selection of a file depends on the shape of the metal, whether it is flat, an edge, a hole, etc.; the kind and hardness of the metal; how much you intend to file; and how fast you intend to do it. A general rule: fine-cut files for edges and hard metals, coarse cuts for soft metals or large shapes. If the file clogs, clean it with a file card or pick out the material with a soft wire; chalking the file teeth will help reduce this problem.

To use a file, grasp it by the handle (yes, file handles really help) and the end, and push down on the work during the forward stroke. Lift the file slightly on the return stroke. This gives the teeth a chance to clean themselves and prevents wear. Long, smooth strokes are the best way to file.

For draw filing, the file is held at both ends and is drawn toward you like a drawknife. This produces a coarser finish, but removes metal faster than the normal filing method.

File for steel; file for aluminum; lead float file.

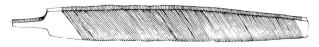

Steel

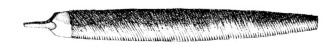

Aluminum

Lead

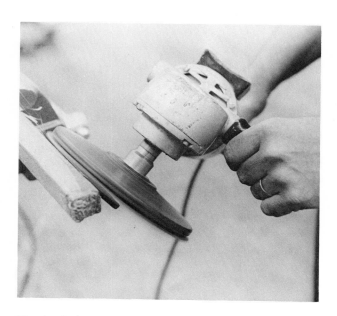

Hand grinder.

To file mild steel use a flat bastard for rapid shaping unless the work is thin. If filing thin steel, use a smooth or second cut. Finish with a smooth. Filing copper or brass requires a sharp file. For filing aluminum there are special files that have coarse, up-set teeth that clog less than regular files; they leave a smooth finish. Lead is filed with a lead float file that has a very sharp, open tooth cut, much like a wood rasp. It cuts rapidly without clogging and leaves a smooth finish.

Remember, whatever the file or the material, several teeth must be on the surface at once. This prevents chattering and tooth breakage, and will make the work easier.

Grinding

Grinding is the removal of metal from the parent stock by an abrasive wheel. Usually the grinding wheel or disk is mounted on a medium-speed motor—either bench-mounted or portable.

Grinding Safety

The operator must wear shatter-proof safety glasses for all grinding operations. If a bench grinder is in use, shatter-proof shields should be used. Loose clothing and hair are dangerous. Beware of setting fires with the sparks.

Grinding Wheels and Their Selection

Grinding wheels are selected by the material to be ground. Aluminum oxide wheels are best for grinding steel; silicon carbide wheels are used for grinding iron, brass and aluminum.

The abrasive in a grinding wheel is held together by various means. The most common is the vitrified bond (also the most versatile and useful for theatrical purposes).

The coarseness of a wheel is given in grain sizes—a type of measurement that indicates that the grains of abrasive passed through a screen with the same number of holes p.s.i. (a #20 grain passed through a screen with 20 holes p.s.i.). Thus finer wheels have higher numbers.

Bench grinders usually have provision for two wheels; it is standard practice to have one coarse wheel and one fine. Portable grinders are usually equipped with a coarse wheel. Disk grinders use replaceable grinding disks of various grades.

Abrasive Cut-Off Disks

Mention should be made of the abrasive cut-off disk. These are fiberglass-reinforced abrasive disks that will fit portable grinders, portable and fixed circular saws, and radial saws. They do a relatively fast job of cutting light angle, bar, rod and tubing. They enable you to adapt standard woodworking machinery to metal cutting without great expense. **Remember to clean out all the sawdust from the machine before using it, or you may cause a fire.** I think a power hacksaw is a better way to cut metal, but if you don't have one, this does a nice job. **Wear goggles and flame-proof clothing.**

Grinder Operation

Operation of a grinder is simple: the metal is brought against the rotating wheel and is held there until the desired amount of stock is removed. Pressure against the wheel should be firm enough to insure cutting but not enough to significantly lower the speed. Friction heat should be controlled by frequent applications of water. Moving the stock back and forth across the wheel will prevent uneven wear.

Uses for Grinders

Grinders are used to prepare steel edges to a vee shape for welding, to smooth off welds, to reduce

Bench grinder.

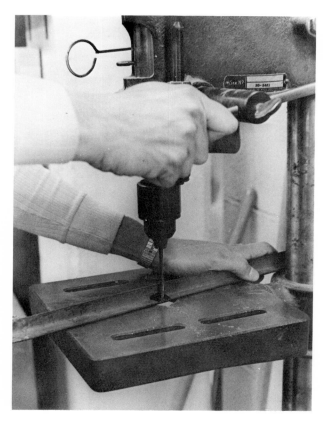
Drill press in use.

parts to correct size and to give a finer finish than is obtainable by sawing or particularly, flamecutting. Grinding can be used for shaping and sharpening various scraping and cutting tools.

Drilling

Drilling metal requires a high-speed steel twist drill that has two cutting edges ground to a standard point angle of 118° and two helical flutes to allow the chips to escape.

Drill Sizes and Lengths

Drills are available in 4 sizes:

Fractions— $\frac{1}{64}''$ to $3\frac{1}{2}''$
Numbers—#1 to #80 (.228″ to .013″)
Letters—A to Z (.234″ to .413″)
Metric

Drill lengths increase with diameter. However, special long-length drills are available: $\frac{1}{16}''$ to $\frac{1}{8}''$ drills are available up to 6″ long, and $\frac{1}{8}''$ to $\frac{1}{4}''$ up to 12″ long.

Speeds and Feeds

Although each drill size has a specific speed for each material, for practical purposes the following guidelines should suffice:

1. The larger the drill, the slower the speed.
2. The harder the material, the slower the speed.
   a. Drill aluminum at high speed.
   b. Drill brass at medium speed.
   c. Drill steel at low speed.

The drill should be fed into the material so that continuous, even cutting will take place. Too slow a feed dulls the drill; too fast a feed will cause hole deflection, drill breakage and machine jamming.

Tools for Drills

Twist drills are held in the chuck of either a drill press or a portable hand drill. For accuracy and ease of working the drill press is preferred; it also has easily adjustable speeds and depth stops—helpful in drilling various materials and parts.

Centerpunching

All holes to be drilled in any metal should be centerpunched. This gives the drill something to "bite" into at the start of the hole and prevents the drill from wandering and breaking. If a large hole is being drilled the circumference should be scribed with dividers, then centerpunched. The center centerpunch mark is drilled with a center drill and the hole is drilled with the larger drill. The centerpunch marks around the circumference allow you to see if the drill is deflecting; if it is, the work should be angled to bring the drill back on true.

Drills Need Lubricants

Lubricants are used to help keep the drill sharp and to prevent undue heating. Soluble oil is suitable for aluminum and brass (if any coolant is needed). Sulfurized oil is good for steel, but cast iron and malleable iron are best drilled dry in the scene shop. In drilling steel never let the drill go dry. Remember to remove the oil when finished—oil and scenery do not mix.

Accurate Drilling

The most accurate way to drill holes in metal is to first centerpunch the hole at its center and then place the work on the drill-press table. Place a center drill in the drill-press chuck. Position the work by lowering the point of the center drill so that it engages the centerpunch mark. With slight downward pressure on the drill, rotate it by hand *backward.* This will accurately align the drill and the

Reamers, straight and helical.

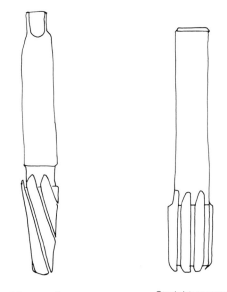

Helical (tapered) reamer   Straight reamer

centerpunch mark. Hold it in this position and clamp the work to the table. Drill the center hole using the appropriate lubricant, remove the center drill, replace with the final-sized drill and complete the hole.

If great accuracy is not needed, just centerpunch and drill with the appropriately sized drill.

Drilling and Reaming

Drilling provides a fast, accurate method of making holes in metal. It does not create stress and cracks in the metal as does punching, and it provides a smoother, more accurate finish than a flamecut hole. If extreme accuracy is needed, as in bearings, drill the hole slightly undersize and use a straight fluted reamer. If a keyway or oil groove is present in the hole, a helical fluted reamer must be used. Remember that a reamer must always be turned in the direction of cutting, even when being removed, to in-

sure good surface finish. Reaming is not necessary for most theatrical uses.

Drilling Safety

1. Wear safety glasses.
2. Do not have loose clothing or hair that might catch in the drill.
3. Remove chuck keys before starting drill.
4. Clamp the work to drill-press table, or at least place it against the column of the machine so it cannot spin if the drill jams.

WARNING: Be particularly careful when trying to enlarge holes in metal with a drill that is slightly larger than the hole. The drill may bind in the hole and cause the work to spin out of control or twist the portable drill out of your hands. To prevent this hazard, use a drill press and clamp the work to its table securely.

Metal Fastening

Once metal has been shaped and cut to the proper size, it is generally fastened. Some of the methods, like bolting, are obvious; others, such as welding, require more detailed explanation.

Bolts

Bolts are designed to draw two or more pieces of material together and hold them by using the mechanical advantage of the screw found in their threads. The bolt is tightened by turning it into a threaded hole in one of the pieces being joined (the piece farthest from the bolt head) or by a nut.

Bolt Classification

Practically speaking, a bolt is typed by its material, style of head, and length and type of thread.

Machine Bolts

Machine bolts are either square or hex-headed with threads on only part of their shank. Their main use is to hold two or more pieces of metal together. The bottom of the head fits tightly against the material. Although square-headed machine bolts are adequate for most theatrical applications, the hex head is more adaptable to socket wrenches and allows more wrench positions for tightening in small places.

Carriage Bolts

Carriage bolts, with their flat oval head and square, antiturning upper shank, are primarily used in wood, preferably hardwood. Their use in metal will result in hole deformity and unnecessary bolt stress unless placed in a hard-to-make square hole. Carriage bolts are only used in metal work where it would be impossible to hold the head with a wrench.

Bolt Threads

The theatre uses bolts with three threading systems: National Coarse, National Fine and Metric.

National Coarse National Coarse is the most common bolt thread in the shop. It uses the largest thread of all three systems—this allows rapid tightening, good reusability in spite of thread damage and resistance to stripping when threaded into softer materials like aluminum and plastic. If the threads become damaged, in a strike for instance, they may be repaired with a die nut. Pounding a bolt from a hole with a brass- or plastic-headed hammer will prevent most damage. With the National Coarse system a ⅜″ bolt will have 16 threads per inch.

National Fine National Fine uses more threads per inch of a given diameter than National Coarse. This gives greater mechanical advantage in tightening; when used in thin materials it allows more threads to hold. National Fine threads resist loosening by vibration, thus are often used in machinery. Remember that the finer threads are more prone to damage than National Coarse. A ⅜″ bolt has 24 threads per inch in National Fine.

Metric The metric system is gradually appearing on bolts in this country. Roughly speaking, metric threads are comparable to National Coarse and National Fine since various pitches are available for a given diameter of bolt. For example, a 6mm diameter bolt can have 0.75 or 1.0 threads per millimeter of length. In larger diameters, say 12mm, you will find pitches of 0.75, 1.0, 1.25, 1.50 and 1.75 threads per mm. When America adopts the metric system, hopefully a few standard sizes and pitches will be used to simplify inventory and reuse.

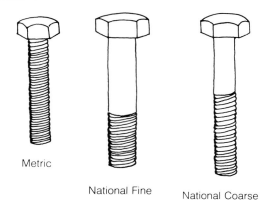

Bolts and threads; metric, National Fine, National Coarse.

Metric

National Fine

National Coarse

Stove Bolts

Stove bolts are usually threaded their entire length and have either a round head or flat countersunk head. Either head can be slotted for a standard screwdriver or a Phillips. Stove bolts can be used to join smaller steel parts other than stoves and are occasionally used in parts of stage equipment.

Machine Screws

Machine screws are basically finely threaded stove bolts used primarily in small stage and shop tools.

Cap Screws

Cap screws are short machine bolts, ¼″ to 1½″ in diameter, that are machined to close tolerances. The threads usually run the full length of the shank. Unistrut fittings are a major use for ½″ cap screws in the theatre.

Sheet Metal Screws

Sheet metal or soft metal may be joined by the sheet metal screw. These are self-threading, require no nuts and can be used in blind fastening situations where access or disassembly may be needed. They are available in a number of standard head types (round, flat, countersunk and pan) and lengths.

Special Purpose Bolts and Screws

There are hundreds of special purpose fasteners. If you have a particular problem that cannot be solved by the use of conventional bolts, nuts or screws, consult the various handbooks and catalogs. An amazing variety of fasteners is available—hopefully you will find something that works and is available for delivery before opening night.

Uses for Bolts

Bolts and machine screws are used for several reasons. Because they use screw threads, they can be used to tighten and hold objects—no other fastener can do such large amounts of tightening as well. They can be secured by the use of lock-washers, double nutting, an aerobic adhesive like Lockite or even by painting. Bolts are used where a joint must be able to come apart, as in stage platforms or the inside of an electric drill. Bolts have an advantage in that they are the simplest fastener to use in metal. It takes little training to teach someone to drill a hole, insert a bolt, and tighten the nut properly. Bolts and nuts are easily salvaged; with little

Sheet metal screws.

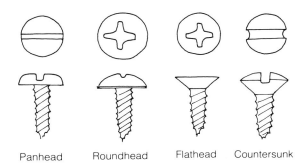

Panhead   Roundhead   Flathead   Countersunk

Tapping.

Die in use.

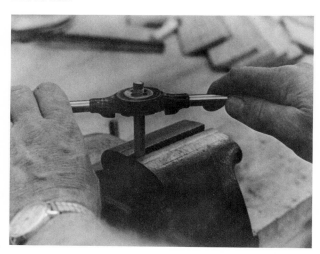

care they can be reused time and time again—something that is unique to this form of fastener.

Threading

Most threading in the theatre is done with a standard tap and die set, available in any reasonably good hardware store. The die is used to thread a bolt or rod. The material has a slight bevel ground or filed on its end and is clamped vertically in a vise. The die, which is secured in its diestock or handle, is placed with its starting side down on the rod. (Most dies are now marked to show the correct starting side; it is the side where the teeth taper inward.) Hold the die level (90° to the rod), press down and turn it clockwise. Use cutting oil. When the die has been engaged for about a turn, reverse direction until you feel the chips break loose. This will make for longer die life and better threading. Continue this process until you have reached the desired length of thread. Spin the die off the rod and clean up.

Taps are used to thread holes. For a given size of tap, the hole must be drilled undersize to allow material for the threads, (as shown in Appendix D). The tap, clamped in its holder, is aligned with the hole and is turned clockwise into it. After each turn, reverse direction to break the chips, as with the die. If the hole does not go all the way through the metal and if threads are needed all the way to the bottom, the threads must be finished with a bottoming tap, since the normal taper of a tap will not complete the job. Make certain to remove all chips from the bottom of the hole before using the bottoming tap. Normally it is easier to drill the hole deeper than necessary so that a standard taper tap can complete enough threads for the job. Spin out the tap when the threading is completed.

Pipes are threaded in a similar fashion with pipe taps and dies.

Rivets

Rivets are nonreusable, permanent fasteners. Basically, a rivet is a single-headed piece of metal rod made from a soft alloy of steel, copper, brass or aluminum that is placed in a hole through two or more pieces of metal and is spread (headed over) to join the pieces and to prevent the rivet from being withdrawn from the hole. Non-ferrous rivets are usually of the *cold set* variety; that is, they are headed over without heating. While some steel rivets are classified as cold set, most are *hot set*: they must be brought to red heat and headed over in that state. These have the advantage of making a tighter joint in steel, for in cooling the rivet contracts enough to make the joint extremely tight. Hot set rivets are not used in aluminum because the temperature of the rivet would harm the temper of the material being riveted.

Pipe die in use.

Heading Over Rivets

Heading over a rivet is done in several ways. One way is to hold the plain "bucking bar" (a large piece of iron or steel which is held against the rivet head to give it sufficient mass so it will not be pounded out of the hole) on the head of the rivet. Pound with a ball-peen hammer or peen the plain end (which should protrude the length of the rivet diameter) into an overlapping rivet head. This is preferred to the cruder technique of pounding the headed end of the rivet and using the plain bucking bar to mash the plain end of the rivet into a rough approximation of a head, often with little shear or tensile strength due to the erratic distribution of the head metal. For really professional riveting, the bucking bar should be formed into a female die of the rivet head; the rivet is then headed over into a precisely shaped head of uniform strength and appearance using a pneumatic riveting hammer.

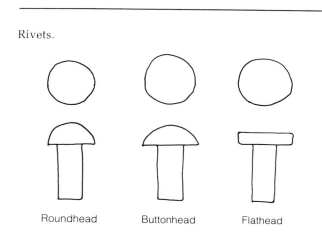

Rivets.

Roundhead   Buttonhead   Flathead

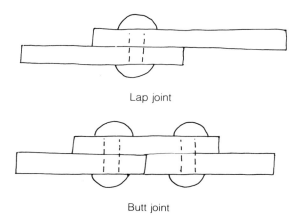

Riveted joints.

Lap joint

Butt joint

Rivet Head Types

Rivets are manufactured in three main head types: the round head is often used in structural work because of its greater head strength; the flat head or tinner's rivet is used mainly in small sizes for sheet metal work; the countersunk, a reverse-conical shaped head, is meant to be used in countersunk holes so that the head is not exposed above the surface of the metal (these are not as strong as the other types).

Riveted Joints

Lap and butt joints are the two main ways of joining metal by riveting. In a lap joint the metal sheets are overlapped and secured by one or two rows of rivets. A butt joint butts the two sheets together and uses a splice plate which is attached to each sheet by one or two rows of rivets. A single rivet joint has one row of rivets on a lap joint or one row on each side of a lap joint. Double riveting uses two rows of rivets at those points.

Whether a joint is butt or lap is determined by the design of the structure. Spacing of the rivets is determined by the strength requirements of the joint. In choosing rivet size, standard practice is to have the rivet diameter fall between 1.2 and 1.4 times the thickness of the plate. The length of the rivet should be long enough to allow it to protrude the length of its diameter beyond the thickness of the material.

Uses for Riveted Joints

In the theatre, riveted joints are used primarily to join aluminum shapes and sheet. These joints require less equipment and training for workers than aluminum welding. In many cases, riveted joints are superior since they do not cause heat distortion or loss of temper that may occur in welding. A riveted joint that is not set tight becomes a simple hinge with many applications such as lighting pantagraphs. Riveting is still a very useful technique.

Pop Rivets and Riveting

Pop rivets are self-heading fasteners; they consist of a hollow tubular rivet with a flat head. A rod passes through the tube and protrudes beyond the flat head. The other end of the rod has an attached ball slightly larger than the rivet tube. To head, grasp the protruding rod in the special hand plier setting tool and place the rivet in a hole in the work so that the bottom face of the rivet head and the outer surface of the work are in direct contact. Squeeze the handle of the setting pliers to pull the ball up through the tubular rivet, which expands. When the ball reaches the limit of its travel by coming up to the material being riveted, the rod snaps off, leaving the expanded rivet in place. These rivets are available in four diameters: $3/32''$, $1/8''$, $5/32''$ and $3/16''$. Lengths vary from $1/8''$ to $1''$, and possibly larger. Steel and aluminum are the common materials.

Pop riveted joints.

Use of Pop Rivets

The advantage of this type of riveting is obvious: It does not need a bucking bar to head the opposite end of the rivet; therefore, it can be used for blind riveting. Tubular shapes can be riveted as well as other structures where it would be impossible to use a bucking bar. Pop rivets and their industrial counterparts can be used where pounding would be harmful. Although they are somewhat more expensive than conventional rivets, they are handy, easy to use and can be used in any lightweight rivet application.

Soldering, Brazing and Welding

Another fastening concept uses a substance that penetrates the surfaces of the two pieces to be fastened to permanently bond them into one. These substances are not reusable and do not retain a distinct shape or form when they have been used, as do screws, bolts and rivets.

Soldering

Metals can be joined by soldering. This is the technique of heating the material until a lower melting-point alloy will flow, penetrating the joint and its surfaces to make a mechanical bond when cool. For most metals used in the theatre, solder is usually a 50/50 mixture of tin and lead; it melts at 421°F, far below the melting points of the metals being joined. Solder for aluminum is generally 60% tin and 30% zinc; it is used at a temperature between 550°F and 770°F because of the high thermal conductivity of aluminum. Other special solders are available in a range of alloys and melting points for both aluminum and other materials. It is possible to assemble a complicated item by making the first joints with a high-temperature solder and the subsequent joints with progressively lower melting-point solders. Any soldering operation that is done below 800°F is called *soft soldering*. Solders are available in bar, wire (either solid or flux-cored) and powder mixed with flux (in some instances).

Soldering Flux

Soldering fluxes are chemicals that perform several necessary functions to allow solder to work. Fluxes clean away oxides on work surfaces that prevent good bonding; they also prevent new oxidation when the metal is heated to soldering temperature. Fluxes act as a sort of metallic detergent because they reduce the surface tension of the molten solder and help it penetrate the heated work surfaces to make a sound joint.

Various fluxes are used for particular metals. For steel, copper and brass, sal ammoniac is good. Galvanized iron is fluxed with muriatic acid. Zinc chloride will work on tin plate, lead and stainless steel. Aluminum requires tin and zinc chloride fluxes. Rosin fluxes are useful in electronics since they require no cleanup as do the other fluxes. Commercial variations are available for all these fluxing materials, usually in solid, liquid and paste form.

Design of Soldered Joints

If you think of solder as a glue, joint design is simple. Solder works best when there is plenty of mating surface area, as in gluing. Telescoping fits, as used in copper pipe joints; sheets of metal that overlap or that are bent into the overlapping hooks of the tinner's seam; wires or rods that are crossed, wrapped around each other or tightly parallel—all these are good joints. Most mechanically sound joints can be successfully reinforced or made leakproof by soldering. Remember, solder cannot make a strong butt joint on small surfaces, as in splicing a thin rod.

Soldering Techniques

Soldering is simple if a few simple rules are observed. First, the materials *must* be clean. All oxides, scale, oil, insulation and paint must be removed by either grinding or sandpapering. If the materials being soldered are not clean, a good solder bond will be next to impossible. Second, a flux is applied. Third, the work must be at a temperature that will melt the solder. If you have soldering equipment with accurate heat control, 535°F is a good working temperature. If the material is not hot enough to melt the solder, it will not penetrate the metal and a cold joint with little or no holding power will result. This is a frequent mistake of the beginner.

When a joint is soldered, the solder first melts. It wets the surfaces of the joint and is drawn by capillary attraction between them. When the heat is removed, the solder cools and solidifies. Do not move the joint until this takes place.

Techniques of Soldering, Use of the Iron

There are two basic methods of soldering for scenic work. The first is the soldering iron technique. The actual tool, a soldering iron, may be: the old fashioned, externally heated soldering copper; an electrically heated soldering iron; or the quick-heat soldering gun. To use any of these, the cool iron tip is cleaned to bare copper, coated with flux, heated to approximately 535°F and given an even coating of solder to prevent the bare copper from oxidizing (thus becoming incapable of holding solder on its surface). The iron is then loaded with molten solder and is touched to a fluxed, clean joint. When enough heat is transferred to the joint, the capillary attraction of the joint will pull the molten solder off the iron and into the crack while additional heat from the iron causes complete penetration of the metal, insuring a good joint. The iron can be run along the seam, joining the pieces and making a fillet of solder as it goes. The fillet can be for slight reinforcement or to fill the joint completely so that it will become invisible after surface finishing. The iron technique is particularly good for any joint which requires shaping of the solder in addition to bonding, or where the parts are too delicate to be exposed to a torch flame. Dents may be filled and surfaces may be textured with this technique.

Torch Soldering Technique

In torch soldering the parts to be joined are cleaned, placed in their proper positions, clamped if necessary and fluxed. The torch, a self-contained propane tank or air-acetylene type, is used to heat the metal around the joint. The flame should never touch the actual joining area since it will burn away the flux and oxidize the metal. When the metal is hot enough to melt solder, the flame is removed and wire solder which has been dipped in flux, or contains a flux core, is applied in a sufficient amount to fill the joint.

Iron soldering.

Torch soldering.

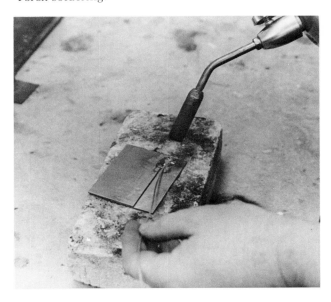

Sweat Soldering Technique

The soldering torch is particularly adaptable to the sweat soldering technique. The pieces to be joined are first tinned (coated) with solder at the actual joining area, recoated with flux, placed in position and heated until the solder melts and joins. This technique is particularly useful when neatness is a prerequisite and no trace of solder is to mar the surfaces. In a variation of this technique (instead of tinning the pieces) they are coated with a solder paste (a ground 50/50 solder in a water-based flux), joined and heated until fusion takes place. This is an excellent technique for small assemblies.

The torch method of soldering is most useful in large work that is too big and heat-conductive for a soldering iron to solder. It is excellent for sweat soldering and can be used with the hard solder alloys that require greater heat.

Aluminum Soldering

Aluminum soldering is a bit more difficult than that of other metals. Aluminum oxide, which forms very quickly on any exposed surface of the metal, does not hold solder. This must be prevented by flux or abrasion, and be stopped from re-forming while the solder is being added to the surface. Also, aluminum is a terrific conductor of heat. It is extremely difficult to keep a large or thick joint up to soldering temperature unless a torch is used. You must be careful not to leave the flame of one of the hotter torches (like oxyacetylene) on one spot too long because you stand a good chance of melting a hole in the work!

Despite these problems, aluminum can be soldered. There are several workable techniques and temperature ranges; I have selected an intermediate temperature process that uses a reaction-type flux of tin chloride and zinc chloride, and a solder of 60% tin and 40% zinc. This will melt at 390°F but will not flow into the joint below 645°F.

Working temperatures will be higher because of the thermal conductivity of aluminum which rapidly dissipates heat.

To solder, first clean the parts with sandpaper until the oxide is removed. Apply the flux in liquid vehicle or dry powder form. Arrange the parts as you want them to be joined and apply the torch. Bring the work up to the proper heat (when the solder is touched to the joint and melts), apply the solder and with the torch direct the heat along the joint so that the solder flows and fills the seam. When this is complete, remove the torch (overheating the joint weakens it), allow the work to cool and then remove the flux by scrubbing in very hot water and detergent. Rinse well and dry.

Abrasion Soldering of Aluminum

Since fluxes may cause corrosion problems, there is a fluxless soldering technique called abrasion soldering. The work is heated to the melting point of the solder; the solder, in stick form, is vigorously rubbed on the surfaces of the joint as it melts. As this is done, the aluminum oxide is scratched away and the clean metal is instantly covered with molten solder which bonds and prevents additional oxidation. A stainless steel brush may help to scrub the surface of the work through the pool of molten solder. When all the joint areas are covered, the pieces are clamped together and the joint is sweat soldered together. This technique is particularly useful for butt or mitered joints where it is difficult to remove flux.

Advantages of Soldering

Soldering of aluminum, steel and other metals is used for several reasons. It can be used to join thin sections of sheet metal that would be difficult to weld since they would melt under the intense heat of the oxyacetylene flame. Soldering does not require the more expensive equipment that is needed for welding. It produces a permanent joint that may be easily removed by simple reheating and cleaning away of the molten solder. This important quality allows the prop person to solder intricate but strong detail onto a metal prop and then successfully remove it for another use. Numerous parts may be soldered together for duplicate machining, thus saving time on many small parts. Soldering is also used for such common operations as joining wires to electronic equipment or fabricating sheet metal. It is the simplest hot metal-joining technique and, next to actual welding, the most useful.

Silver soldering.

Hard or Silver Soldering

Soldering that takes place above 800°F but below 1,200°F with no melting of the actual work is called hard soldering. Usually this is done with a solder containing various amounts of silver, copper and zinc—an alloy called silver solder. Properly made, silver-soldered joints are strong, can stand considerably more heat than soft-soldered ones and resist vibration. They are the strongest of the solders. Aluminum cannot be soldered with these solders because of its high melting point.

Silver Solders

There is quite a range of silver solders or silver brazing alloys available. Melting points vary from about 1,150°F to 1,620°F. For some solders, like Braze It, there is a 150° temperature increase above its melting point needed to make the solder flow into a joint. Others, like Eutectic, will flow almost as soon as they melt. Strip and wire are the best forms of these solders for theatre use.

Oxyacetylene welding.

Silver Soldering Techniques

Any joint that is a good slide fit can be silver soldered. Technically, it should have between .002″ and .004″ clearance to give the solder room to penetrate. Due to the cost of solder and the fact that it does not make a strong filler, avoid loose joints and poor fit-up. The joint is cleaned with sandpaper, coated with silver-solder flux (borax in some form) and heated. When the work is the proper temperature, touch a fluxed piece of solder to the joint; it should melt and ultimately flow into the crack. Use the torch to work this flow along the joint until soldering is complete. Do not overheat. Some people like to cut pieces of solder, flux them, place them along the joint and heat the whole business until the solder flows; this too is an acceptable technique. When the joint has cooled after soldering, the flux may be removed with hot water and scrubbing.

Brazing

Brazing, the technique of joining metals with an alloy of brass, is quite similar to hard soldering except that the brazing alloy does not flow as easily. The rules of metal cleanliness, use of specialized fluxes and heat transfer apply. The main difference lies in the higher melting points, working temperatures and final joint strength. Since brazing usually requires the heat of an oxyacetylene torch, I will discuss the technique after examining oxyacetylene processes and equipment.

Welding

Welding is the most spectacular and effective permanent metal joining process of practical value for the theatre. The basic principle of welding is complete fusion of the joining pieces: melting them into one another to make a permanent joint. Although the process is basically simple, there are several problems that must be overcome to produce a sound and permanent weld. The first is to provide enough heat to melt the pieces into one another. For our purposes this is provided by either specialized oxyacetylene or arc welding equipment. The second problem is to prevent the molten metal from oxidizing or nitrogenating (absorbing oxygen or nitrogen from the atmostphere) which produces detrimental weld characteristics. This is prevented by the chemically neutral oxyacetylene flame or a gaseous shield created from the burning flux of the arc electrode. The third difficulty in welding is the placement of the molten metal, particularly the filler metal for the weld seam. This is done by careful manipulation of the welding tools and materials controlled by the welder.

Oxygen tanks.

Oxyacetylene Equipment

Oxyacetylene welding requires special equipment.

Oxyacetylene Tanks

The basic tool of oxyacetylene welding is the flame produced from commercially pure oxygen and acetylene. This combination of gases, when burning properly, has an approximate temperature of 6,000° F—enough heat to melt all commercial metals. For theatrical use these two gases are bought in steel cylinders under tremendous pressure.

Oxygen Cylinders

Oxygen cylinders are usually green and have a top mounted valve with a right-hand thread for the oxygen regulator. The tanks are filled with oxygen at 2,200 p.s.i. at 70°F when full. A 9″ x 56″ cylinder contains 244 cu. ft. of oxygen; a 7″ x 48″ contains

Acetylene tanks.

122 cu. ft.; a 7″ x 35″ holds 80 cu. ft. Oxygen cylinders are not sold but are rented from a supplier after a 30-day grace period. To avoid this demurrage, it is possible to buy the ownership of a cylinder which, when empty, may be traded for a full one. Then you are only charged for the oxygen.

Acetylene Cylinders

Acetylene gas is dangerously unstable at pressures above 15 p.s.i. To safely store a usable volume in the acetylene cylinder, the gas must be dissolved in acetone, allowing a safe pressure of 225 p.s.i. The cylinder is packed with a porous material that has been soaked in acetone. The top of the cylinder is usually recessed to protect the special wrench- (key-) operated valve. The connection threads are left handed to prevent confusion with oxygen equipment. The most common sizes of acetylene cylinders hold 60, 100 and 300 cu. ft. at 225 p.s.i.

The Oxygen Regulator

Since oxygen in the cylinder is at 2,200 p.s.i. and welding seldom requires pressures above 70 p.s.i., a regulator is necessary to control the pressure supplied to the actual welding. To maintain a constant working pressure, even though the pressure in the cylinder is declining, the regulator must have a sensitive controlling mechanism in addition to a reducing valve. This must be adjustable because the various welding operations require various pressures. Simply explained, this regulation is accomplished by means of an adjustable diaphragm controlled by an adjustment screw. The tighter the screw, the greater the pressure that is allowed to pass. A single-stage regulator reduces the tank pressure to working pressure in one operation. A two-stage regulator reduces the pressure before it contacts the final regulation diaphragm in order to have finer adjustments. For the purposes of scenic work, the single-stage regulator is adequate. Externally the regulator consists of the adjustment screw, the outlet connection (threaded right hand), the tank pressure gauge, a delivered pressure gauge and a right-hand threaded intake connection. On the oxygen regulator, the tank gauge is calibrated up to 3,000 p.s.i.; the delivery gauge reads from 1 to 100 p.s.i.

The Acetylene Regulator

Internally the acetylene regulator is the same as the oxygen although it is built to withstand the lower pressure of the acetylene cylinder. The tank gauge is calibrated from 1 to 350 p.s.i.; the delivery gauge is from 1 to 15 p.s.i. The connections are left-hand threaded.

The Delivery Hose

A hose connects the regulators to the torch. Special dual-passage hose should be used. The red side is for the acetylene, the green for the oxygen. The end of each hose should have the properly threaded connections to fit the regulators and the torch. Only welding hose should be used since other types often disintegrate after contact with the gas. Twenty-five feet is a good, usable length for a scene shop.

The Welding Torch

The welding torch has three primary functions: it mixes the oxygen and acetylene to form a correct mixture for proper combustion; it regulates the size of the flame by the interchangeable combustion tips; it provides a convenient, safe way to hold the flame. Oxygen and acetylene pass through the torch's control valves, through tubes in the handle and enter the mixing chamber. There they are combined and the mixture travels through the goose neck to the tip where it is ignited and burned.

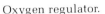

Oxygen regulator.

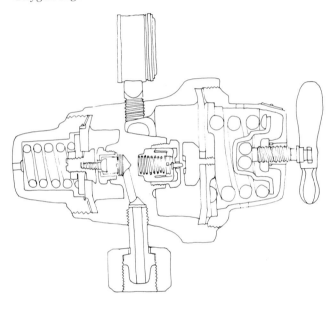

Welding torch.

Cutting torch.

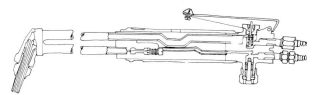

There are many types of torches on the market. You need only use one—a medium-duty, balanced-flow type. It will provide enough heat to weld up to 2″ plate. Balanced flow means that the gas pressures are equal (as with regulated gases from a tank source). The torch is provided with a variety of interchangeable welding and heating tips so that it may be used for a wide range of operations.

The Cutting Attachment

The cutting attachment is designed to take the place of a welding head on a medium-duty, balanced-flow torch body. The principle of flamecutting is to heat the steel red hot and to then burn it away with a stream of pure oxygen. Cutting torches and attachments provide this stream of pure oxygen that does the cutting, and small oxyacetylene flames that preheat and keep the steel at a temperature to facilitate proper cutting. The preheated flames are controlled much as welding torches are. The cutting oxygen is controlled by a lever on the side of the attachment. Except for the addition of this feature, the cutting attachment is basically the same as the torch.

Goggles

Welding goggles must be considered part of basic oxyacetylene equipment. They protect the operator's eyes from excessive glare and hot-metal splash. They enable the welder to accurately see what is happening to the work in progress. There are several types of goggle housings—some of which will fit over glasses. Interchangeable lenses may be inserted as necessary; the larger the welding flame, the darker the lens should be.

Gloves

Leather gloves are a must for safe welding. Not only do they protect the hands from direct heat radiation but also from direct contact with hot material. Gauntlet cuffs are desirable since they protect the welder's wrists, prevent shirt cuffs from burning and tend to discourage hot metal from splashing into the gloves.

Striker

Friction strikers are the best way to light a torch. Matches should <u>never</u> be used—the igniting gas may burn a hand and the matches might catch fire in the welder's pocket from the heat of the work. Only slight amounts of acetylene should be released for lighting; just "crack" the valve open. Some welders like to use a lighted candle set on the bench when the work requires much re-lighting and shutting off.

The Welding Cart

This is not necessary for welding that is done in an area easily reached by a length of welding hose, as long as the tanks are chained in a stable, upright position to a wall or workbench. However, when you must move the oxyacetylene equipment to different locations, it is indispensable. Not only does it provide a safe way to move and store the tanks and equipment without dismantling, but it can carry all the other welding supplies as well. The cart can be commercial or homemade. Remember, it must be large enough to safely carry the equipment but small enough to negotiate the various doors and passages of your theatre!

Welding Rods

Welding or filler rods supply the metal to fill the bevels in the material being welded. Their standard length is 36″ and they are available in diameters from $^1/_{16}$″ to $^3/_8$″. Rods should have alloys corresponding to the metal being welded. Cast iron and aluminum rods are available for welding those materials.

Lighting the torch.

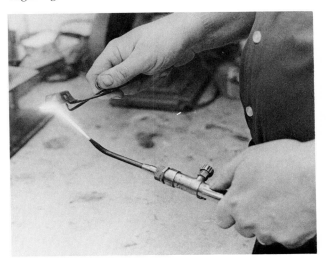

For additional information regarding welding equipment, refer to the bibliography or to catalogues of the various manufacturers.

Welding Techniques

Setting Up Equipment Be sure that the oxygen and acetylene tanks have been chained in place on a welding cart and that their protective caps have been removed. Wipe out the seats of each valve and then quickly open and close them to blow out any dirt that may be there. Attach the regulators with the proper size wrench, make certain the regulator adjustment screws are screwed out and loose and then turn on the tanks. Oxygen is turned on all the way; acetylene is only opened 1½ turns; the wrench or key is left on the tank in case of emergency. Attach the hoses and the torch.

Lighting The Torch To light the torch follow this sequence of operations:

1. Make certain all valves on the torch are off and all connections are tight.
2. Open the acetylene valve on the torch one full turn. Screw in the acetylene regulator screw until the gas escapes from the torch at the proper working pressure. Shut off the acetylene valve on the torch quickly.
3. Repeat this process with the oxygen regulator and oxygen valve on the torch.
4. Open the acetylene valve slightly and use a striker to light the torch. **Make sure you are wearing gloves.**
5. Open the torch acetylene valve until the flame is no longer producing free carbon particles or smoke, and is making a slight roaring sound.
6. Open the torch oxygen valve slowly until the torch is producing a neutral flame (see below). You are ready to begin heating or welding.

The Neutral Flame

Since the neutral flame is the basis for most torch operations, additional information is in order. As oxygen is added to an acetylene flame an inner white, cone-shaped flame will form at the torch tip. At first it will have a feathery edge. This is a carburizing flame that will add free carbon to the molten metal and make it brittle. As more oxygen is added, the feathery edge will disappear, leaving only the slightly rounded, white inner cone of flame. This is the neutral flame which, because it is chemically neutral, is used for most torch operations. Adding additional oxygen will produce a smaller, sharp-tipped, inner cone of flame. This is an oxidizing flame that will burn the molten metal. (Note the illustrations.)

The Gas Pressures

The proper working gas pressures should be determined by the charts supplied with the welding and cutting tips. Different brands of equipment use different pressures. Basically, in welding, the oxygen and acetylene pressures should be equal, with the larger tips receiving greater pressures than the smaller in proportion to their size.

Shutting Off Equipment

To shut off the welding equipment, follow these steps:

1. Turn off the torch oxygen valve, then the acetylene valve. (This is all one has to do to turn off the torch for a few minutes.)
2. Turn off both tanks.
3. Open the torch oxygen valve until both oxygen gauges on the regulator read "O." Unscrew the oxygen regulator adjustment screw and turn off the torch oxygen.
4. Repeat the process for the acetylene.
5. Coil hose neatly, clean up and leave.

Material Preparation

Before the actual welding begins, the materials must be properly prepared. All joints must be cleaned. Oil, grease, paint, rust, scale and dirt must be removed by sanding, grinding or chemical removers. The joint does not have to be as clean as required for soldering. All oil and lubricants must be removed from aluminum before welding.

Edge Preparation

Since the heat of the welding flame will only penetrate to a certain depth (depending on its size and the thickness of the material) it may be necessary to prepare the edges that will be welded so there can be complete penetration of the metal, resulting in a sound weld. For steel up to $3/16''$ thick no edge preparation is needed. Plan the fit-up of the work so that there is a gap that is between $3/32''$ and $1/8''$ wide between the parts. This will allow complete penetration of the weld. For steel $3/16''$ to $5/8''$ thick, grind the edges to a single vee at an approximate angle of 60°. The beveled pieces should be placed with a slight gap between them, as in working with thinner steel. Weld only on the beveled side. On the chance that you might weld $1/2''$ or thicker steel, a double vee is used; this will be welded on both sides. Plug welds are prepared by drilling holes through the top piece of the joint. One-half inch diameter is good for this. Remember: all vees, holes and cracks should be filled in the welding.

Types of Welds

Most welding will have joints that fall under the classification of butt, flange, lap, fillet or plug welds. While most are used for a specific, standard joint, occasional problem situations may require a combination of these to produce a satisfactory joint. Remember, the edges of the material should always be prepared as discussed.

Four types of flame; acetylene, carbonizing, neutral, oxidizing.

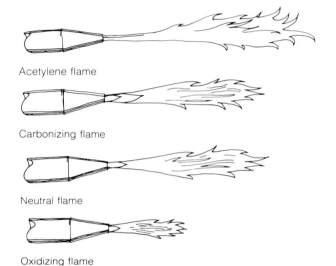

Acetylene flame

Carbonizing flame

Neutral flame

Oxidizing flame

Joints, single vee and double vee.

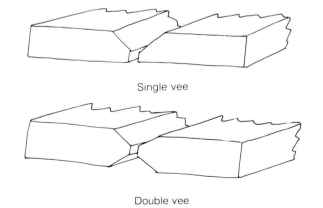

Single vee

Double vee

Butt weld

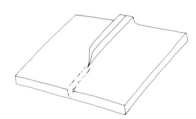

Flange weld

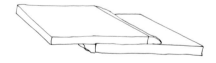

Lap weld

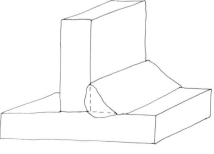

Fillet weld

The Butt Weld   The butt weld is the simplest joint. This weld is between two pieces lined up with each other on the same plane with no overlap. It is the most economical weld since it requires the minimum of material and welding supplies. It is one of the strongest metal joints.

The Flange Weld   The flange weld is used for joining sheet metal. The joint is prepared by bending a small flange at the edge of each piece. These are butted together and melted by torch into a weld that is practically flush with the surface—often with no additional filler rod. The upstruck part to the flange should equal the thickness of the material. Clamping the sheets will produce a weld that will remain flat.

The Lap Weld   The lap weld is used to join two overlapping steel sheets (as in a situation where bolts or rivets could be used). The weld runs along the edge of the plates. It is important to weld the overlapping edge on both sides of the work because a single weld has little resistance to bending in this type of joint. The lap weld requires twice the welding as a good butt joint to achieve the same strength. Do not use it unless you have to.

The Fillet Weld   Fillet welds are used when a piece of material joins another continuous piece at an angle somewhere between the ends. The weld metal is deposited so that it forms a fillet in the corner of the joint. As in the lap joint, both sides should be welded if one-side welding cannot afford complete penetration.

The Plug Weld   The plug weld is a simple, neat way to join overlapping pieces when you do not want to weld the edges. Holes are drilled in the top piece and the bottom part is welded to the top through the hole. The weld metal fills the hole. After grinding it is hard to tell where the weld was made. The plug weld is best when strength requirements are moderate and neatness is a must.

Plug weld

Oxyacetylene Forehand Welding Technique

Having discussed the properties of the welded joint and types of welds, we turn to basic oxyacetylene welding techniques. For simplicity, assume that the weld is a single vee, flat butt joint in ¼″ steel plate. Vertical, horizontal and overhead welding are variations of this process.

The welder holds the torch in one hand and the ⅛″ mild steel welding rod in the other. Until the steel at the end of the bevel begins to melt, the torch is held ½″ away and vertical to the bevel. When the metal becomes red hot and the surfaces of the bevel begin to melt and glisten, the torch angle is changed to about 45° and the actual welding is begun. To forehand weld, the torch is pointed in the direction of welding and the rod precedes the torch. To distribute the heat and the weld metal, the torch and rod are oscillated in opposite, semi-circular paths. This heats the whole bevel to the melting point so that the welding puddle will fuse with it as metal is melted from the rod. Note that two things are happening. First, the molten steel from the rod is filling the bottom of the bevel for about ½″. Then the bevel is filled to the top and the welding is moved forward another ½″. To do this, first create a molten puddle of steel at the bottom of the bevel. Aim the torch at the edges just in front of the puddle. Hold the rod out of the puddle, but keep it hot in the edges of the flame. When the edges of the bevel begin to melt, add metal from the rod to fill the bottom of the bevel. Then move the puddle over this area with the rod. This will fill up about half the bevel's depth. Then, with rod and flame, move the puddle back to where it was to finish filling the bevel slightly above the surface of the steel. The torch is then moved forward and the process repeated down the joint until the weld is complete. Try to create an advancing slope of weld with the molten pool of metal being pushed up and down it, depositing metal as it is moved. Remember, a neutral flame is used throughout.

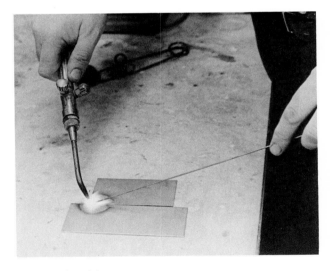
Forehand welding.

Forehand Pointers

There are five points to remember in forehand welding:

1. There must be complete melting and penetration to the bottom of the joint.
2. The inner cone of the welding flame must not touch the rod to cause carbonization.
3. The filler rod must add enough metal to entirely fill the joint.
4. The filler metal should be evenly deposited; the sides of the weld bead should be parallel with no gaps or holes.
5. A neutral flame *must* be used at all times.

Use of Forehand Welding

In forehand welding the rod prevents the flame from directly heating the bottom of the bevel just ahead of the advancing weld puddle. On thin metal this is an advantage because it keeps the torch from melting through the thin bottom of the bevel. This is not so for thicker (3/8" and up) sections since the rod must be kept higher above the bevel to insure heat penetration. This increases the chances of the filler metal becoming oxidized or burned since it is not shielded well by the neutral atmosphere of the flame. The forehand technique is also used in brazing.

Backhand Welding

Backhand welding is useful for welding thicker material. The torch is pointed back at the start of the weld and the rod is manipulated between it and the weld. The start of the vee is·heated to the melting point while the rod is preheated in the outer edge of the neutral flame. As soon as the end of the bevel begins to melt, the rod is added to make a puddle. Keep the end of the rod in the puddle, and move it slightly along the bevel, filling its bottom. Do not do this until the surface of the bevel has begun to melt. Once this is done, direct the flame onto the rod, and

Backhand welding.

move the rod backward to fill the first part of the bevel up to the surface of the work. When complete, move the rod and puddle back to the bottom of the vee and repeat the process until the weld is complete.

Backhand Pointers

1. Obtain complete fusion between the edges of the plate and the weld puddle.
2. Use a more plastic puddle than in forehand welding.
3. Use a narrower vee angle than in forehand welding.
4. Direct the welding flame on the edges of the vee without sideward motion.
5. Always use a neutral flame.

Use of Backhand Welding

When correctly performed, backhand welding easily accomplishes complete weld fusion and penetration, particularly on material that is more than ¼" thick. It requires a narrower vee angle, it does not oxidize (since the puddle is better protected by the shielding, chemically neutral flame), and results in a more ductile weld. Backhand welding can produce a sound joint faster than an equivalent forehand weld of the same quality.

Oxyacetylene Welding in Non-Flat Positions

Although it is easier to weld with the work in a flat position, it is possible to produce good welds at other angles. This is particularly useful when you are assembling a steel set and can no longer turn the work so that all welding will be in the flat position.

The trick in non-flat oxyacetylene welding is in the control of the puddle of molten metal. By varying the angle and distance of the torch from it, you can control the fluidity and direction of flow. Try to make it liquid to fuse with the melted edges of the joint, but then allow it to cool slightly into a mushy, plastic state that will stay put. In overhead welding the puddle can be quite liquid as long as it does not form drops which quickly fall in a hot, unpleasant shower of molten metal. Try to work with a thin, filmlike puddle in these circumstances.

Vertical Welding

To weld vertically with the forehand technique, start at the bottom of the vee with the torch angled up at about 45°. This will vary during the welding in order to push the puddle into place with gas pressure and to vary the heat. Heat the bottom of the joint until it begins to melt and add some rod. Work the puddle up the vee to fill it, then slightly reheat what you have already done until its surface is again molten. Work the puddle back down on this area until it is level with the surface. Do not let the puddle get too fluid or it will run out of the weld. When that part of the weld is level with the surface of the work, redirect the flame to the vee above it, and repeat the process until the weld is complete. Try to keep the puddle plastic so it flows only when manipulated by the flame or the rod and make certain that the areas it is worked over are molten. This will insure a sound weld.

Vertical joints can be welded by the backhand technique. The process is similar to flat welding except that using the backhand method you weld down the joint, using the pressure of the escaping gas flame to hold back the puddle and to prevent it from running over unheated metal. This is a bit difficult for beginners to master.

Horizontal Oxyacetylene Welding

A horizontal joint is a seam parallel with the floor but on a vertical surface. It may be welded by either the forehand or backhand technique as in flat position welding. The main difference is that the flame

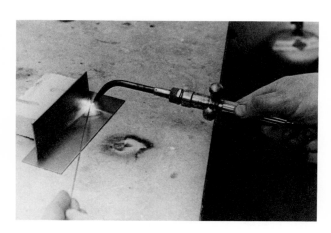

Oxyacetylene fillet welding.

should be directed at the lower piece of the joint to prevent the upper part from melting too quickly (heat rises). Try to build up a ledge on the lower piece to hold the puddle as you weld.

Overhead Oxyacetylene Welding

In overhead welding the flame is pointed into the vee at almost a 90° angle. This will help prevent both too much area from being heated and the formation of molten metal drops. Otherwise, it is practically the same as either forehand or backhand welding (if you can imagine flat welding while standing on your head!) It is hard to work above your head, and you will tire quickly during overhead welding. I try to avoid it whenever possible.

Fillet Welding

In welding the fillet-type joint, there is a tendency for the vertical plate to melt and run down before the horizontal one is at welding temperature. This prevents a sound weld. To avoid this common occurrence, direct the flame mostly on the lower piece, get it hot first; then bring the vertical part up to welding temperature. Using either the forehand or backhand technique, the flame should be angled to heat the lower part and should lead or trail about 45°. Manipulate the rod and torch to produce a nice fillet of weld metal. Make certain it has fused all the way to the corner of the joint.

Plug Welds

To weld a plug weld, make certain the bottom and edges of the hole are molten before adding filler rod. Since a relatively small area is welded in this type of joint, it is important that the entire hole be filled with a sound weld. The surface of the weld may be ground flush when it has cooled to produce an invisible joint.

Brazing

The use of the torch for brazing is quite similar to that of forehand welding except that the flame should be carbonizing just slightly. Also, use a flux-coated brazing rod instead of steel welding rod. The steel being joined by this technique is heated only to a low red heat before the brazing puddle is applied. The puddle can be controlled by the rod and by torch manipulation. Remember that brazing does not melt the work; it is more like a high-temperature solder.

Uses for Brazing

Brazing is useful for joining thin sheets of steel where the heat of welding might cause holes from melting, or to joint brass or cast iron, neither of which can be joined with steel welding. Brazing can be used to join galvanized sheet and malleable iron without harming their characteristics. It can also be used to join heavy sections where the intense heat of welding (2,700°F) would cause excessive warping not found in the lower brazing temperature of 1,600°F. Brazing is an easy way to join lightweight steel tubing. Many pieces of furniture and lightweight yet strong railings can be assembled easily by brazing.

Oxyacetylene Welding for Aluminum

Don't! If you must try, consult the various welding manuals listed in the bibliography. The inert gas forms of arc welding do such a superior job that most people have given up oxyacetylene aluminum welding. It is difficult, and the results are usually awful.

Flamecutting

Red hot steel will burn when a stream of pure oxygen is directed on it. Oxyacetylene flamecutting utilizes this principle.

Flamecutting.

Flamecutting Equipment The main distinction of oxyacetylene flamecutting equipment is that a cutting torch is substituted for a welding tip. All other oxyacetylene equipment remains the same. Unlike the welding torch, which has a single passage for oxygen and acetylene, the cutting torch has an additional tube for pure oxygen. This is controlled by a lever on the side of the torch body. The mixed oxygen and acetylene burn at 4 to 6 orifices on the cutting tip, and the pure oxygen is released through a central hole.

Operation The preheat flames should be lit and adjusted to a neutral flame. These are used to heat the steel red hot, the tip kept about ½″ from the metal. When red heat has been reached, the torch is lifted slightly back and the oxygen lever is pushed in all the way. The pure oxygen burns a hole in the plate. The torch is slightly slanted in the direction of the cut and is moved along the cutting line (soapstone is best for marking this) at a speed that gives a smooth cut. Too fast a speed will result in the oxygen hitting unheated metal and thus stopping the cut. If this occurs, release the oxygen lever until the steel is reheated sufficiently to start again. Too slow a speed results in a wide, messy cut with unnecessary slag along the bottom edges of the work. Straight edges help make smoother cuts.

Oxygen pressures for cutting are always 3 or 4 times those of the acetylene. Equipment specifications should be consulted for the correct pressures for the thickness of steel being cut.

Flamecutting provides a quick, easy way to cut steel when a fine-finished edge is not desired. It is particularly useful for cutting odd shapes, or during a dismantling operation or strike. Remember: only steel and some forms of iron may be cut by this process.

Oxyacetylene Safety We have now covered the basic techniques, principles and materials of oxyacetylene brazing, welding and cutting. Like regular shop equipment, when used safely, they can be useful tools for the technician. Used carelessly they can be lethal and burn down the theatre. Before we progress further, it is time to give the rules of oxyacetylene welding and cutting safety.

1. **Allow no oil to contact any oxyacetylene equipment. Explosion may result.**
2. **Keep heat away from cylinders.**
3. **Since acetylene is unstable above 15 p.s.i., don't try to use it above that pressure.**
4. **Wear flameproofed clothing with no areas exposed that could catch sparks.**
5. **Wear leather shoes and gloves. Wear goggles with the proper density filterplate.**
6. **Test all equipment for leaks periodically.**
7. **Beware of flammable material in the welding area. Cover all flammable material (such as a wooden floor) with asbestos or other fireproofed material when it is not practical to work elsewhere. Have a pressurized-water extinguisher handy.**
8. **Follow equipment instructions TO THE LETTER.**
9. **Use a striker or candle for torch lighting; never use matches.**
10. **Have adequate ventilation, particularly when welding or cutting galvanized material. Drink whole milk before working on galvanized stock—it will prevent you from becoming ill.**
11. **When cutting, look out for falling pieces.**
12. **Do not cut or weld a container that has held a flammable substance without first completely cleaning it.**
13. **Use common sense.**

Arc Welding for Steel

Principles of Arc Welding The electric arc is the hottest available heat source easily obtainable commercially. Harnessing of this arc makes electric arc welding possible. In this fusion technique, a welding circuit is generated by a welding transformer or generator. The work is made part of this circuit by connecting it by a ground cable to the power source; the circuit is completed by the cable connecting the electrode holder to the transformer. By contacting the "positive" electrode to the "negative" work, an intense arc of 13,000°F is created which melts the work almost instantly. As the arc is moved along a seam, it fuses the metal and supplies additional filler metal from the electrode itself.

The Arc and Electrode   As the heat of the arc melts both the work and the electrode, tiny globules of metal are formed on the end of the electrode. These are picked up by the arc stream traveling into the molten pool of steel on the work and are deposited there. It is the force of the arc stream that will deposit the filler material—even in an overhead position. As in oxyacetylene welding, this molten metal has great affinity for oxygen and nitrogen, both of which cause defects in the final weld. In order to prevent absorption of these gases, the electrodes should be covered with a coating of flux, which burns away under the arc and creates a shielding neutral atmosphere around the molten metal, thus preventing oxidation and nitrogenating. As the metal cools, this flux forms a protective slag that must be chipped away if more welding is to be done.

Arc Welding Equipment   Although there are many kinds of equipment and materials for arc welding available, I shall describe only the equipment I feel is suitable for general use in the theatre.

The Welding Transformer   I have found that the AC 220 amp, 240 volt, static transformer utility welder is ideal for most scene shop uses. AC arc

Arc welding.

Welding transformer.

welding is a great deal easier to master than DC and the machine itself is simpler and cheaper. The AC welding transformers can produce currents from as low as 20 amps to their maximum of 220 amps in two ways. Some use a system of multiple taps in the reactor coil. These terminate in various arrangements of jacks on the face of the machine; the plugs on the end of the welding cables can be connected in various ways to give the desired current rating. Although this type is simple and has no moving parts to get out of order, it does have a slight disadvantage of only supplying amperage in 10-amp intervals. Some machines use a multi-position rotary switch instead of the jacks. The other method of varying the amperage is to use a crank and screw or a slider to move the iron core in and out of the reactor coil; this varies the air gap in it which varies the reactance of the coil and gives continuous adjustment to the output current of this form of transformer welder.

The Connection Cables Electrode and ground cables must be tough enough to withstand rough usage, be of sufficient size (usually #2) to carry the 220 amp current at least 12′ and be flexible for effective welder movement. These requirements are met in rubber-covered, multi-strand, super-flexible copper cable.

The Connections and the Electrode Holder The ground cable should be connected to the work or to the welding bench by a copper, spring-closing grounding clamp. This is preferred to the lug found on many ground cables since the welding equipment will be used in a variety of locations and will not be bolted to the welding bench.

The electrode holder can be one of many types. Basically it is a copper clamp that connects the electrode to the welding cable. The electrode holder should be insulated totally from the electrode except on the protected clamping surfaces. These jaws should allow the electrode to be held in a variety of positions. There should be some type of heat shielding for the welder's hand. Although there are many heavy-duty electrode holders available, don't buy one that is rated above the capacity of your welding equipment since the larger types get heavy and the inexperienced welder often has difficulty maintaining effective control and balance of movement as a result.

The Welding Hood   Since the electric arc creates an intense light, splatters metal and emits strong ultraviolet rays, a protective shield and eye filter are necessary, both for safety and to be able to see what you are doing. These shields are made in two types—the hood, usually worn by the welder, and the hand-held type, usually used by the helper. A good shield will have an adjustable head band, changeable filters that may be lifted out of sight without raising the hood and be lightweight. I recommend the fiberglass helmets.

The filter plate in every helmet and shield is protected by a piece of clear glass on the welding side. This is soon pocked by splattering metal and should be replaced when it interferes with good working vision. Since using these clear glass plates is considerably cheaper than replacing filter plates, they should always be used.

The filter plates are rated in shades of darkness, increasing in density from #8 to #14. #10 is adequate for a 220 amp welder; #12 is preferred for heli-arc. Replacement plates should always be on hand.

Gloves   Leather gauntlet gloves are a must.

Clothing   Heavy, flameproofed clothing must be worn when arc welding. There should be no place sparks can catch; pants should cover boot tops; shirt necks should button up. Exposed skin can contract nasty sunburn from the ultraviolet rays of the arc as well as burns from the splattering metal.

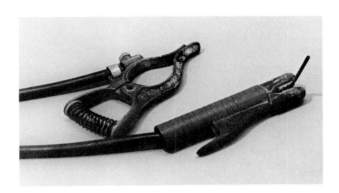

Grounding clamp and electrode holder.

Hoods and chipping hammer.

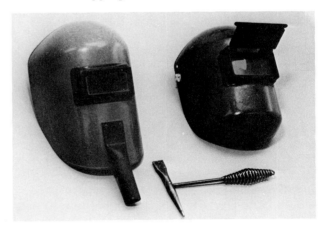

The Electrodes The electrodes are the expendable unit in arc welding equipment. They serve two functions: they carry the arc and supply filler material to the weld. In AC welding, electrodes are a steel rod of varying alloy that is flux-coated. Since there are many kinds of electrodes, here are 7 basic points to help you determine which type to use:

1. What type of current is to be used for welding? (AC in most theatrical situations)
2. How thick is the metal you are going to weld?
3. How clean is the metal; how tight is the fit-up; are the joints veed out, etc.?
4. What type of welding do the joints require—flat, horizontal or vertical?
5. What position will you weld in—flat, horizontal, vertical or overhead?
6. What special physical requirements will the joint require—extra strength, ductility, hardness, etc.?
7. What shape do you want the weld to be—flat, convex or concave?

Electrode Characteristics The many types of electrodes have widely differing uses and characteristics. They are classified by a numbering system devised by the American Welding Society (AWS) and the American Society for Testing Materials (ASTM). The number of each electrode tells a great deal about it. For example:

E7014

The E stands for electrode (i.e., suitable for arc welding)

70, the first two digits, indicate strength in 1,000 p.s.i. or, in this case, 70,000 p.s.i.

1, the third digit, indicates the position of welding. 1 is all-position, 2 is flat or horizontal and 3 is flat only.

4 indicates the type of welding (AC, +DC, –DC). When read with the third digit, it will also indicate the type of flux. Numbers 11, 12, 13, 14, 16, 18 and 24 are common electrodes that may be used with an AC welder. Numbers 14 and 24 have iron power in their flux which makes them particularly easy to use.

The following types of electrodes have been selected because they are adaptable to AC welding and are useful for the type of metal work done in the scene shop.

E6011 The E6011 electrode is usable in all positions, although it is superior for making vertical and overhead fillet and butt welds. The deposited metal has high elongation values, great strength and is corrosion resistant. The flux is a heavy coating, low in materials. It produces little slag, relying on gases for protection of the molten metal. The arc is stable and very penetrating, excellent for tight fit-up with little or no veeing. It should be used with a medium-long arc for best results.

E7014 The E7014, called Easyarc by one manufacturer, is usable for all positions but, unlike the E6011, has low penetration. This makes it useful for welding thin sheet metal and joints that have very poor fit-up. It is great for filling holes and building up surfaces. The iron powder in the flux makes it easy to strike an arc and aids in the flow of weld metal. Although the E7014 may be used by dragging it along the weld line, better results are obtained when a short, visible arc is used.

E7024 The E7024, popularly called Drag rod, can be used only for flat or horizontal welding. It has a heavy, iron-powder flux that is so thick that the electrode may be used by resting it on its flux and dragging it along the weld line. This makes it particularly useful for beginning welders. It produces good root fusion in horizontal fillets and will fill poorly fitted joints.

These three types of electrodes will handle most arc welding problems.

Electrode Diameter The diameter of a given electrode for a specific weld depends on the thickness of the material and the skill of the operator. A general rule is to use an electrode whose diameter is the same as the thickness of the work—up to ⅜", the largest electrode available. This does not apply when the joint is overhead, horizontal or vertical because the effect of gravity overcomes the force of the arc and causes poorer joining when the large sizes of electrodes are used. In these situations ³/₁₆" electrodes are the largest which should be used.

Since the larger electrodes deposit weld metal much faster than the smaller ones, use the largest allowable electrode for each particular weld situation. Practically speaking, a stock of ¹/₁₆", ⅛" and some ⁵/₃₂" will weld almost anything you may require, even if it takes multiple passes to finish the welds on thicker material.

Material Distortion

Since the intense heat of the arc melts relatively small amounts of metal and heats less of the total mass to a flexible, plastic state than oxyacetylene welding, there are considerably more stresses set up within the work by the cooling of the arc-welded metal. These stresses will result in distortion of the finished work. To prevent this, the parts of the work should be firmly clamped before welding and not released until after the weld has cooled. Often it helps to peen (hammer lightly) the weld as it cools to relieve stress. Tack welding the ends of long welds is another good method for preventing distortion and simplifing the clamping setup. It is helpful to design the welds by setting up opposing forces that cancel each other out.

Use of Patterns and Jigs

Many layout jobs on metal can be done quickly and more accurately by first making thin wooden patterns for each piece. Joint fit-up can be checked and

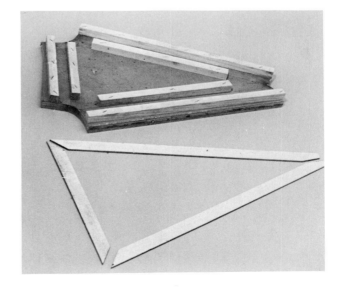

Jigs and wooden patterns.

cutting lines quickly traced on the metal by using patterns. Final size can be checked by comparing piece and pattern.

In welding repetitive assemblies, such as stair treads, facilitate the work by welding the pieces in a jig. This holds the parts in their exact placement and helps prevent warpage. The jig should be cut away from the corners where the welding is to be done; this prevents setting the jig on fire. Longer production runs could use a steel jig. Jigs are also useful for repetitive bends, such as a double veed butt weld.

Arc Welding—Flat Position

For the following example, assume that we are welding ¼″ mild steel plate that has been veed out on one side for a butt joint. We are using an ⅛″ E7024 electrode and the welding transformer is set for 130 amp output.

Clamp the electrode in the holder and lower it in a vertical position to ½″ above one end of the vee. Lower your filter plate and touch the electrode end to the work with a quick, scratching motion. As soon as the arc starts, raise the electrode slightly above the work (about ¹/₃₂″ to maintain the arc). Although this type of electrode may be used by dragging it along the vee, better work will result if a short arc is used. You may have trouble with the electrode sticking to the work. If this happens, do not panic, just quickly twist it loose or, that failing, release it from the electrode holder and free it by hand with a cold chisel. Do not become discouraged if this happens—it takes practice to overcome it.

When the arc is making its characteristic frying sound you are ready to weld down the seam. Keep the electrode perpendicular to the work laterally so that you will deposit equal amounts of filler material on each side of the joint. Allow the end of the electrode to trail slightly as you weld down the vee. This will allow the slag and gases in the joint to wash up

Rotary motion of the electrode.

to the surface of the molten puddle of metal and help produce a better joint. With a slight circular movement, work the arcing electrode down the vee, building up the rippled weld bead behind. The speed of this operation should be fast enough to keep the puddle of melted steel behind the arc, since it will otherwise absorb the penetrating force of the arc stream and perhaps cause electrode sticking. When you have worked your way to the end of the vee, push the electrode into the work (almost to the sticking point) and then slowly pull it away, leaving a sharp, definite end to your weld. Allow the weld to cool and chip off the slag.

Your newly deposited bead of weld metal should show complete penetration, have a uniform cross section and have a smoothly rippled bead pattern with no evidence of undercutting, overlapping or piling up of excessive weld metal.

The flat seam presents the basic technique for arc welding. It is possible to weld an adequately strong joint in this position after less than an hour's instruction. Most welds should be placed in this position, if possible, because it is the easiest to do.

Cleaning and Rewelding   If the single bead did not bring the level of the weld up to the surface of the work, additional beads must be deposited. Before this can be done, all traces of slag and oxide must be chipped off the bead with the chipping hammer and then wirebrushed. This is important, for if it is not done the finished seam will develop internal cracks because the impurities prevented complete fusion between the additional beads— weld failure.

Arc Welding Pointers

1. Use electrodes of the proper grade and diameter for the job: E7024 for flat position, E6011 for vertical and overhead positions and E7014 for all positions.
2. Properly clean and prepare the metal to be welded.

Unchipped vs. chipped weld.

3. Use the correct amperage setting to produce the right amount of heat. This is determined by the thickness of the work and the electrode diameter. Check your welder's instructions for specific information.
4. Maintain the correct arc length.
5. Move the arc at the correct speed along the weld.
6. Feed the electrode into the arc at the correct speed.
7. Start, restart, and fill the arc craters correctly.
8. Remove the slag before any rewelding.

Horizontal Arc Welding For horizontal arc welding (welding a joint that is on a vertical surface, but parallel with the floor) it is best to use an E7014 electrode with about 10 amps less current than you would use if the joint were flat. The electrode should be held perpendicular to the work with the tip trailing slightly. Use a shorter arc with the tip of the electrode closer to the surface of the work than in flat welding. This prevents the puddle from flowing out of the vee before it solidifies. All other flat welding techniques apply.

In preparing the seam for horizontal welding it is helpful to grind a slight bevel on the lower piece. This provides a shelf for the molten metal to penetrate and keeps it from flowing by gravity onto unheated metal. If multiple beads are required, try to maintain this shelf until the final filling bead.

Vertical Arc Welding Vertical joints are best welded from bottom to top since any metal that escapes from the puddle will only run over what has been welded, and will not cover unwelded material. An E6011 or E7014 electrode should be used. This will be held perpendicular to the joint, but the tip will be inclined upward slightly—about 5°. This is the only case where the tip leads instead of trails in welding.

Start your arc at the bottom of the vee. As soon as a puddle develops, rock the electrode up the vee about ¼". This will heat the next portion of the joint to be welded and allow the deposited metal below to cool so it will not run out of the vee. Rock the electrode back down, deposit more metal, rock it back up a little farther along the joint and so on until you finish. Remember not to break the arc while rocking back and forth. The process should be quick enough to keep building a ledge of newly deposited metal to support the hotter puddle. You may have to work faster and use higher amperage than in horizontal welding.

Overhead Arc Welding Overhead welding is the most difficult position to master. It is physically tiring for the welder; it is unpleasant (due to the shower of sparks and slag) and the influence of gravity is directly opposed to the disposition of the weld metal.

Since, in this example, we are welding on ¼" plate, an E6011, $^5/_{32}$" diameter electrode will be used. Clamp it in the angle position in the electrode holder to allow greater wrist movement with less discomfort. Loop the welding cable around your shoulder to take its weight off your hand and arm.

Use the same sort of rocking motion that you did for vertical welding. Work quickly so you do not form metal drops which fall. Use slightly more amperage and a slightly shorter arc than in vertical welding. Exact settings will have to be determined for yourself. The electrode should be held vertically across the joint and rocked back and forth along the weld line.

Avoid overhead arc welding whenever possible.

Applications for Arc Welding Arc welding is the easiest welding technique to master. It is often used for general run-of-the-shop welding. Unlike oxyacetylene it requires no preheat time and does not constitute a hazard by requiring tanks of flammable gases in the building.

Although the arc is hotter than the oxyacetylene flame, it is not as useful for straight heating and shaping applications since the intense heat is far too localized to be of much value. Compared with the carbon arc torch the oxyacetylene equipment can perform far better because it heats a larger area faster.

The arc is particularly useful for welding large pieces of steel when the considerable preheat time of oxyacetylene would cause warpage or the convection of heat to unwanted areas. Arc requires practically no set-up time and works quickly. Arc welding equipment is considerably more rugged than oxyacetylene items. There are no delicate diaphragms, gauges, or valves to wear or get out of order. Unfortunately, the cutting process, which uses special nichrome electrodes, is not as good as the oxyacetylene cutting torch. Thus, both types of welding equipment are needed in the well-equipped scene shop.

Arc Welding Safety   Although electric arc welding is not unduly dangerous, the following common sense rules and safety practices should be followed:

1. **Do not weld in an area where there are flammable gases or liquids.**
2. **Wear the welding helmet with the correct shade lens plate when you are welding.**
3. **Keep sleeves rolled down and wear leather gloves to prevent radiation and contact burns.**
4. **Never weld in a damp area. Ground your welder.**
5. **Have adequate ventilation. Beware of toxic fumes.**
6. **Keep equipment in good condition. Beware of frayed wire or electrode holder insulation.**
7. **Do not weld containers which have held combustible materials without prior proper cleaning.**

Spot welder.

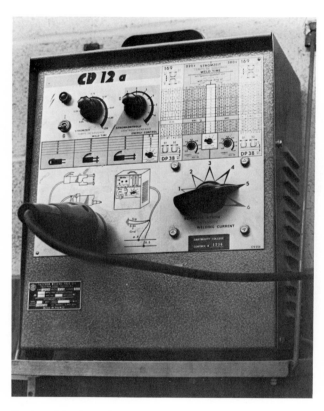

Spot welder transformer.

8. **Do not touch the electrode when you are grounded. Do not touch others with it.**
9. **Warn others not to look at the arc without eye protection.**

Spot Welding The beginning welder may have warpage and melt-through problems when welding thin sheet, wire, or rod with either the oxyacetylene or the arc. Perhaps you wish to weld these materials with a minimum of distortion and little or no evidence of welding. In both cases spot welding may be the answer.

The principle of spot welding is simple. You have an electrode on either side of the joint. These are used to press the joint together, hold it and then create a brief, timed arc between the parts that will melt a spot on each piece. The pressure of the electrodes presses the two molten puddles together, they solidify almost instantly and the spot weld is complete. This process works well for crossing wires and rods as well as lap-type joints on sheet metal. Mild and stainless steel may be spot welded.

Spot Welding Equipment Although spot welders vary in detail and complexity, all use a pair of copper electrodes that can be clamped on each side of the joint. A welding transformer is connected to these and various controls are included to regulate the pressure of the electrodes, the intensity and length of time of the arc and when the timing will start. The simpler machines are fine for theatrical use.

Joint Design for Spot Welding Any simple lap, coach (a lap joint with two 90° flanges that are welded together) or strapped butt joint that can be tightly clamped together by the electrodes may be spot welded. Avoid lock seams and tubing since the current path does not go directly from electrode to electrode and will not make a sound joint. For best results, remember that the lapped pieces must fit tightly and be clean.

To Weld Determine the settings of the intensity (amperage) of the arc, the length of time of the arc and, if your machine has them, the adjustments that control the pressure of the electrodes. Hold the timer from starting until the full welding current flows. This is useful for welding less-than-clean material. All these adjustments are best made by consulting the directions for your particular spot welder and, ultimately, by experience. Don't be afraid to try trial welds on scrap before the real thing. When everything is set, clamp the material lightly between the electrodes, check the placement of the pieces and squeeze the trigger or step on the pedal to fire the welding current. Hold until the weld is complete—the timer will shut off the current at the proper time. To weld a seam, move the electrodes down the joint and repeat.

Spot Welding Pointers

1. Always make certain that the electrodes are in line, tip to tip, and parallel to each other. This creates the best spot welding.
2. The electrode tip diameter should be slightly greater than the thickness of the sheet it contacts. Remember that when you are spot welding unequal thicknesses of sheet you will have unequal electrode diameters.
3. Distance between spot welds (for instance, on a seam) should be about twice the thickness of the metal. If the welds are too close the current will not flow correctly and poor welds will result.
4. Do not spot weld too near the edges of sheet. The molten metal will oxidize (there is no flux or flame to protect it) and the edge of the sheet will burn away. Keep welds back from the edges twice the thickness plus .19″ minimum.
5. Just because you do not see the arc don't forget that spot welds are HOT.

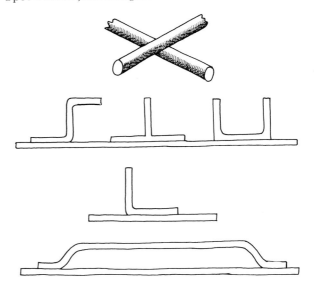

Spot welded joint designs.

Uses Spot welding is one of the best ways to weld light sheet metal, wire and rod without warpage and melt-through problems. If you use these materials often in your shop a spot welder would be a good investment. They are simple to use, once they are properly adjusted to the work, and the results are superior.

Arc Welding Aluminum

There are two major problems in welding aluminum: oxide formation and heat dissipation. Aluminum oxide forms on most aluminum surfaces almost instantly when they are exposed to air. It prevents good welding because it melts at 3,600°F while the metal itself melts at 1,200°F. When you solder aluminum, the oxide may be removed by scraping the surface under a shielding puddle of solder, but the higher temperatures of welding make this technique impractical. The oxide may be removed chemically, but complete cleaning after welding is required, and this takes a lot of time and effort.

Heat dissipation is the other problem. To weld the same thickness aluminum as steel, one needs about 2½ times more heat. The welding transformers must be considerably larger for aluminum welding in spite of the relatively low melting point of the metal.

Oxide removal and high-heat dissipation have been solved by an arc welding process known as heli-arc. The arc and the puddle of molten aluminum are surrounded by a shielding cloud of inert gas. This gaseous shield, usually argon, prevents oxidation of the metal while it is being welded and totally takes the place of fluxes and other chemicals that require cleanup. The welds are attractive and ready for painting, if desired, when they have cooled.

TIG and MIG

An arc with a gaseous shield is used in two basic ways. The first is TIG, or more completely, Tungsten Inert Gas welding (occasionally known as GTA, or Gas Tungsten Arc). In this process the electrode is a non-consumable tungsten rod which, when connected to a stabilized AC welding transformer, creates an arc at the surface of the aluminum without quite touching it. The electrode holder feeds out a stream of shielding gas and if the work requires more than 200 amperes of welding current the holder is cooled by circulating water. Since the aluminum is melted by the arc, which is controlled by one hand of the welder, an aluminum welding rod is fed into the puddle with the other hand. The joint is then welded much the same as in forehand oxy-acetylene work. Although this requires more operator skill and training, TIG is the most versatile of the shielded gas processes for aluminum. It may be used in any position and will weld most thicknesses of aluminum that would be used for scenery or stage equipment. The power supply can also be used for AC welding on steel using the familiar coated electrodes. Since this equipment will cost in excess of $1,000 you could save by not having to buy a conventional welding transformer for your steel welding.

The other process is MIG or Metal Inert Gas welding. Here a positive-polarity direct current is fed to a consumable electrode. This provides its own filler material as well as support of the arc. It is protected by a gaseous shield that comes from the electrode holder. The electrode is actually a roll of wire, aluminum for aluminum welding or steel for steel welding, that is automatically fed through the holder and into the arc as fast as it is used up. One-handed operation is quite possible. MIG is best used on aluminum more then ⅛" thick. It is a much faster process than TIG and requires much less operator skill when everything is properly adjusted. MIG is also ideal for quick, clean welding of steel. Since the shielding gas replaces the flux on the electrode no cleanup is required.

TIG Equipment—Power Supply   The ideal power supply for TIG would be an AC-DC, 300 ampere unit able to weld almost any kind of metal. However, since TIG welding of aluminum requires AC current, and we use primarily steel and aluminum in theatrical applications, the cheaper, stabilized-arc AC machine will do. 300 amperes would not be too large. This AC power supply is not the simple utility welder; the current it produces has a high-voltage, high-frequency current superimposed on it. This prevents the arc from extinguishing as the cycles reverse and facilitates easy arc starting without touching the aluminum. (Touching contaminates the electrode.) Remember that with AC, welding only takes place during the positive half of the cycle. The negative half gives good cleaning action of the oxides and tends to cool the tungsten electrode. TIG power supplies also have built-in valves that control the flow of the shielding gas and cooling water (if used) for the electrode holder. These are usually designed to trigger automatically when welding starts. A foot pedal may be used to control the amperage during welding.

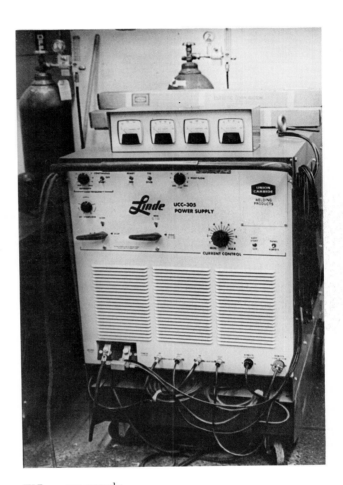

TIG power supply.

Inert Gas Supply

Argon is the usual shielding gas for aluminum welding. It provides good cleaning action and requires less arc voltage than helium (which has a nasty tendency to float away). Argon is supplied in tanks similar to oxygen, and these are usually mounted on the back of the power supply. Gas is fed into the power supply through a regulator that controls its pressure and flow.

TIG system.

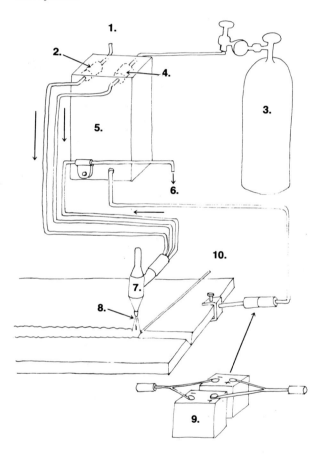

1. Cooling water input
2. Water control solenoid
3. Shielding inert gas
4. Gas control solenoid
5. AC power source
6. Cooling water output
7. TIG torch
8. Tungsten electrode
9. Battery bias (if needed)
10. Filler rod

TIG Electrode Holders   Welding that requires 200 amps or less may need an air-cooled electrode holder. However, the more versatile water-cooled version is preferred. Both hold the non-consumable tungsten electrode in a cup-shaped device in which the gas lens is located. This is connected to the argon tank, and places the shielding gas around the electrode and the molten aluminum. Cooling water circulates within the larger electrode holders to prevent the intense heat of the arc from destroying them. Some electrode holders, or "torches" as they are called, have swivel joints at their heads which make them easier to use in any position.

TIG Electrodes   The non-consumable electrode is a tungsten rod or an alloy of it. They are usually $\frac{1}{16}''$ to $\frac{5}{32}''$ in diameter, depending on the thickness of the materials being welded. Electrodes are prepared for welding aluminum by grinding them lengthwise to a point (crosswise grinding will cause the arc to wander) and then the point is "balled" by striking the arc on a copper block. The electrode should be placed in the torch so it protrudes the distance equal to its diameter. This distance allows a good arc that is protected by the argon shield.

TIG Filler Rods   TIG filler rods are similar in form to those used in oxyacetylene welding. For aluminum, they are usually an improved alloy of that metal. Degassing and deoxidizing materials are usually included in their composition. The size of the filler rod should roughly match the thickness of the material you are welding.

TIG Safety   Since both TIG and MIG are arc welding processes, you must wear the standard arc hood, leather gloves and be suitably dressed for welding. A slightly darker filter plate is recommended since the welding takes place at considerably higher amperages than those used for steel. Remember that aluminum does not have to show a color to be dangerously hot. Wear

gloves and test-touch before reaching for any TIG or MIG work: that will save a lot of burned fingers.

TIG Welding—Flat Position   We will be welding, in this example, a flat butt joint on ¹/₁₆″ aluminum sheet. The material has been degreased and is clamped in position to the welding bench. This will prevent warpage and will provide a backup plate in the weld area. This is needed because, unlike steel, aluminum of this thickness will tend to melt through as you heat the joint to welding temperature. The backup plate acts as a sort of mold to keep the aluminum in place, prevents undue oxidation of the rear surface by preventing much air contact and will act as a heatsink. By consulting the tables provided with the 300 amp, AC-DC TIG unit, set the machine to AC, set the gas flow meter on the argon tank to about 15 cu. ft. per hour and adjust the time-delay switch in the gas line to run for approximately 4 seconds after the arc stops. Amperage is set to the remote-high position since it will be controlled by the foot pedal. The circulating water is turned on to cool the torch. The torch has been equipped with a ¹/₁₆″ tungsten electrode, properly ground and balled on the end, and the proper gas cap. The foot control switch is placed conveniently on the floor under the bench.

Find a comfortable position (a stool helps) and hold a ¹/₁₆″ filler rod in one hand, the torch in the other and a foot on the pedal-controller. Drop the hood over your face and place the torch perpendicular to the end of the joint so the tip of the electrode is about ⅛″ above the work surface. Press down on the pedal slightly and watch the high-frequency AC arc jump to the surface. Keep the torch straight up and press down on the pedal until you have an arc hot enough to melt a small puddle of aluminum. Note that the metal merely melts, without much warning, unlike steel. You may have to move the torch in a small circle as you melt your puddle. Once you have a puddle, tip the torch back about

TIG electrode showing grinding pattern and balling.

TIG electrode and filler rod.

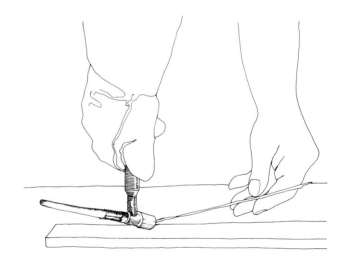

15° from vertical and move it back to the starting edge of the joint. Add some filler rod to the puddle, holding it at about 15° from the work, then remove the rod and bring the torch back down the weld to the leading edge of the puddle. The work will melt slightly ahead of the puddle as you do this and the molten aluminum will flow into it. Repeat this process of heating, backing up the torch slightly, adding the filler rod, pulling out the rod and moving the torch farther along the weld until the joint is complete. You may find that you will have to ease up on the pedal to reduce the amperage of the arc as the work heats up as you weld. In many ways TIG welding is like forehand oxyacetylene welding. The molten aluminum behaves somewhat like solder—it will flow where you direct the heat.

Do not become discouraged if you get into trouble with your early TIG welding. It takes a lot of practice to do it automatically. And remember—it is only metal!

TIG Pointers

1. Read and follow the instructions for your particular unit. You can't fake it!
2. Never touch the tungsten electrode to the work of filler rod. This will contaminate the electrode and prevent good welding. If this happens, stop welding and cut off the contaminated end, regrind the point, reball and start over.
3. Use only enough amperage to get a nice, molten puddle. Extra power will cause melt-through problems.
4. Keep the torch at the proper distance from the work to maintain the arc and the argon gas shield.
5. Let the puddle melt the filler rod, not the arc.
6. Use backing plates for welding thin stock.

TIG Vertical Butt Welds   Vertical butt welds are made in much the same manner as the flat ones, but with two major differences. First, keep the torch perpendicular to the work. This will keep the puddle small and allow deep penetration. Second, weld from top to bottom, feeding the filler rod from the bottom at a 15° angle to the work. Remember, keep the puddle as small as possible so it won't drop out of the weld.

TIG Lap Welds   To do a TIG lap weld, first create a puddle next to the joint on the bottom sheet. When it is liquid, circle the torch up over the top edge of the overlapping piece so the puddle on the bottom and the overlapping edge fuse. It is possible to make this joint without filler rod, but its use will definitely speed the welding. Remember to dip the rod into the puddle, withdraw it and move the arc forward. Repeat until the weld is complete.

TIG Edge and Corner Welds   These are the easiest TIG joints. Clamp the material into position and carefully run the torch along the edge, creating a puddle that fuses the two pieces together. Be careful not to go too slow, or the puddle will run off the edge. Too fast, and the results will be poor fusion and a lumpy edge. The same process is used on flange welding where the upturned edges of thin sheet are melted flush with the flat surface of the work.

TIG Fillet Welds   The technique used to make fillet welds on aluminum with TIG is much the same as that used for the lap weld. The torch is directed more toward the bottom piece since it usually has more mass and because heat tends to rise into the upper part. Use enough filler rod to obtain a nicely shaped fillet.

MIG Equipment   MIG equipment has several important differences from TIG. First, the MIG power supply will only produce DC current. Second, an electrode feeding mechanism is provided. This will

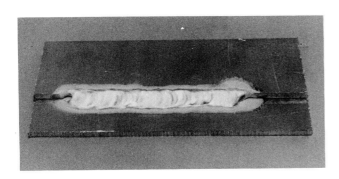

TIG lap weld.

TIG corner weld.

TIG fillet weld.

Wire feed on MIG welder.

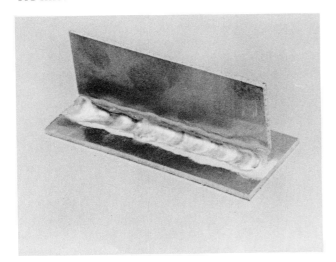

MIG system.

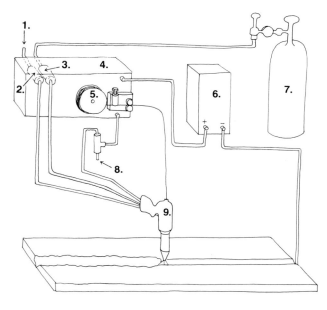

1. Cooling water input
2. Water control solenoid
3. Inert gas control solenoid
4. Wire feed unit
5. MIG electrode
6. DC power source
7. Inert gas for shielding
8. Water output
9. MIG torch

feed interchangeable spools of wire electrode through the cables and hoses to the MIG torch. This is done at a predetermined speed that is a function of the arc voltage—thus synchronizing the feed rate and consumption of the electrode. Various guide rolls and collets in the torch must be changed to accommodate each size of wire. The wire feed will not start until an arc is struck.

Since the MIG electrode wire can only be pushed through the hoses for about 15′, you may encounter problems in getting the torch to the work, particularly in the scene shop. Hobart makes a wire feed mechanism that may be placed near the work while the MIG power supply and gas feed may remain some distance away. These are still controlled by the MIG torch's trigger.

Another company makes an MIG torch that has its own small reel of electrode wire inside itself. While one has the convenience of a short feed length, the torch is a bit bulky and heavy for beginners to use. It is portable, however.

The gas shielding and water cooling processes are much the same as for TIG.

MIG Welding

Most MIG welding for the theatre will use the short arc technique. In this the consumable electrode actually fuses itself to the work, short circuits and melts away with an arc only to repeat the process about 100 times per second. Actual metal transfer takes place in the fusion, not in the arc. Therefore, the process is completely adaptable to welding in any position. Compared to the spray arc technique which is used on heavy materials, the short arc uses lower currents, lower voltages and smaller electrodes. It is ideal for welding the relatively thin materials used in theatre with minimal distortion.

To short arc weld aluminum with MIG first set all the controls on your machine to the settings specified by the instructions for the thickness of the material you are welding. Like TIG, you cannot fake this. Most joints will not require any edge preparation because of the high penetration of the reverse polarity DC current used in the process. The aluminum must be clean, the oxide removed in the welding zone and degreased. If a weld requires more than one pass to complete, it should be cleaned with a stainless steel wire brush before re-welding to remove the oxide layers that have formed.

Flat Position Butt Welding with MIG The aluminum pieces are clamped in place. Fit-up should be reasonably tight. The MIG equipment is properly set. Start at one end of the joint and weld with the forehand technique (electrode leading, end ahead of the torch). You will find that the weld will go very quickly, almost 15″ per minute on .050″ sheet. You will just have to run the torch along the weld line with no oscillation. If all the controls were properly set, you should have made a good weld. The hardest part about it will be setting the feed rate and moving the torch steadily along the joint for an even bead.

Other Short Arc Welds Vertical MIG short arc welds are welded from top to bottom with the torch perpendicular to the work. Fillet welds may be welded by the backhand technique if you find that to be easier.

Spray Arc MIG For welding heavier materials, like ¼″ aluminum plate, the spray arc technique is useful. Here the weld metal is continuously deposited and the electrode never touches the work to short circuit. This takes considerably more welding current and produces much more heat due to the continuous arc. Backup strips are usually required to prevent melt-through of ¼″ to ½″ aluminum. The forehand technique is used in all positions.

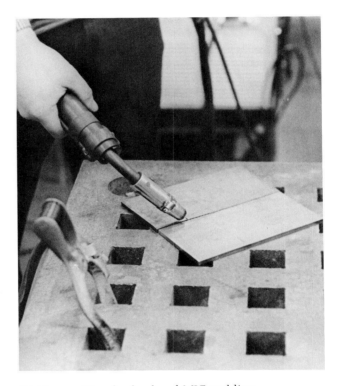

Welder position for forehand MIG welding.

MIG and TIG Conclusions Both MIG and TIG produce superior welds on aluminum. Although the techniques require practice, as do other welding processes, they can be mastered. Mild and stainless steel may also be welded. In fact, MIG welding of mild steel is extremely easy. You just run the torch along the joint and it welds—or so it seems.

The great disadvantage of both TIG and MIG is the cost of the equipment. Both processes require sophisticated machines. A typical MIG unit for theatre use costs around $2,000.00 (1978); TIG units are somewhat cheaper. Unless you are doing a lot of aluminum work, or can justify the cost of the equipment for its educational value, you will probably have to farm out the work to a commercial welding shop. On the other hand, if you can find the money, nothing welds as well as TIG or MIG.

Gluing and Structural Adhesives

Fastening Metal By Gluing

Gluing or bonding metal provides an easy method of repair or fabrication when used within the specialized conditions specified by the manufacturer. There is a tendency to expect the bonded part to act as if it were welded. This can happen if industrial grade adhesives and the proper joint designs are used. Do-it-yourself epoxys are also good—when used correctly.

Types of Adhesion Glue bonds wood by penetrating the minute spaces between the fibers. When dry, the glue forms a hard, strong material that holds the two surfaces together by a mechanical interlocking action.

Unlike wood gluing, metal bonding relies on the attractions between the molecules of the adhesive and the material being bonded. The molecules of the adhesive adhere to the surfaces of the joining parts and generate sufficient molecular attraction or cohesive force to form a stable interface (glue layer) between the surfaces. If the correct adhesive has been chosen, properly applied and allowed to dry (cure), the joint may be so strong that the parent material will fail before the bonded layer.

Types of Adhesives—Contact Cements Contact cements are made from elastomeric materials such as neoprene or natural rubber. These are dissolved in a solvent and added to some long-chain thermoplastic resins. This compound forms an extremely sticky coating when applied to each part and bonds on contact. Strength is gained by aging and by mild heat-curing under pressure. The joint seldom becomes rock hard and will usually have slight cold-flow under shear and heat. Aside from this limitation, contact cements are valuable for general adhesive uses particularly when there are large surfaces between the bonded parts. Sheet metal may be bonded to plywood by this method. Remember, with most contact cements, make certain the parts are properly aligned before placing the pieces together. Contact cements grab quickly and misalignment is almost impossible to correct. Slip-sheets may be useful. Follow their directions.

Cyanoacrylates Cyanoacrylates are thin, clear liquids that are fantastic adhesives. They may be used to bond any metal that has a smooth, grease-free surface and tightly fitting joints. Cyanoacrylates are applied by dropper or applicator bottle, either to separate pieces or directly into the joint by capillary attraction. With slight pressure the material polymerizes or sets. Setting time may be seconds or minutes depending on the formulation of the cyanoacrylate. The strength of the bond will increase with aging—a steel-to-steel bond may reach a strength of more than 3,400 p.s.i. in several days' time.

Cyanoacrylate bonds are reasonably stable but they may be weakened by heat (above 176°F), some solvents (like acetone, acids, alkalines) and in some cases by prolonged contact with moisture. The specifications of each brand should be checked to see what type will fill your need.

WARNING: Cyanoacrylates have a particularly strong attraction to the human skin. Do not get the material on your fingers and then touch them together—instant bonding will result that may require surgical separation. Wear safety glasses while using them—getting cyanoacrylate in your eye and then blinking could have the same result.

Epoxys   Epoxys are generally resins that will react with a catalyst or hardener to form an extremely strong bond that will cure without fumes or evaporation. This makes it one of the best structural adhesives. Epoxys are available in many forms and literally hundreds of formulas. They usually require relatively good fit-up, a reasonable amount of bonding area and minimal clamping pressure to make their strongest bonds. Tensile strengths of about 10,000 p.s.i. have been obtained.

Generally, the hardware-store variety of epoxy will be adequate for most theatrical use. Most manufacturers make industrial epoxy as well, and can be consulted for unusual bonding problems.

General Rules for Structural Adhesives

1. Chemically clean surfaces are a must.
2. Etched surfaces, prepared by chemical or mechanical means, increase the bond strength.
3. Proper mixture, both in method and in amounts, is critical.
4. Thin glue lines resulting from good fit-up are desirable.
5. Avoid skin contact with adhesive. Wash after use.
6. Do not contaminate epoxy resins or catalysts either with foreign matter or each other.

Structural adhesives are a useful adjunct to conventional metal-joining techniques. They are particularly useful in repair of items that heat would damage and where conventional fasteners are not possible or desired. They are not a miracle cure-all, but when used properly give good results.

7

Starting a Metal Program

Shop Space

The development of a theatrical metalworking program requires adequate, well-lit, well-ventilated, fireproofed space. Ideally, this would be a large separate shop on the same level as the stage. There would be clear access to both the stage and the loading dock. This dream shop would contain a full complement of tools, separate welding booths and generous amounts of space for fabrication and material storage. It would be a shop devoted exclusively to metalworking.

This is not usually the case. Since most theatres were built before the development of theatrical metalworking, often the new facilities must be crowded into an already bulging building. Probably the best location for a minimal shop would be in the traproom, provided that adequate ventilation and an exhaust fan with a duct to the outside could be provided. The basic equipment may be placed in a small cage for security, and the actual work may be lifted from the room through the overhead trapped floor. While this facility is far from ideal, it is adequate for most needs. Make sure the shop can meet the local fire code.

Equipment Suggestions

The following list of various types of metalworking equipment does not include costs. There are 3 lists: the absolute minimum, the moderate, and the ideal. Other items can be added depending on your particular needs and desires.

Minimal Metalworking Equipment

Oxyacetylene welding and cutting outfit
Propane soldering outfit
Ballpeen hammer
Hand sledge hammer
Channel lock pliers
4 C clamps
Hand hacksaw and blades
½″ reversible power drill with speed control
Pump-type oilcan
Pipe cutter
Set of pipe dies and stock
Two 18″ pipe wrenches
Heavy-duty vise
High-speed drill index
Three assorted files
Safety glasses
Welding gloves and goggles
Torch tip cleaners
Hand wire brush
Portable disk sander/grinder

Moderate Metalworking Equipment

All items on the minimal list
220 amp AC arc welder
½″ multi-speed drill press.
Power hacksaw
2 visegrip spring clamps
2 pipe-type cabinet clamps
Tap and die set, metric included
Bench grinder with standard wheels
Anvil and supporting block
Pop rivet set
Assorted files
Pipe vise on tripod
Grinding wheel dressing tool
Extra arc welding hoods
Extra pairs of oxyacetylene goggles

Extra welding gloves
Heating tip for torch
Additional oxyacetylene welding and cutting tips
Welding cart for oxyacetylene outfit
Metal bender and dies
Chipping hammer
Automatic centerpunch

Ideal Metalworking Equipment

All items on the minimal and moderate lists
TIG welding outfit
MIG welding outfit
Metal shear
Metal brake
Multi-speed metal-cutting bandsaw with blade welder
Spot welder
Unishear
Nibbler
Electric rivet hammer
Metal lathe
Vertical mill

Storage rack.

Storage Space

Adequate and convenient storage is important. There should be wall racks of adequate size to hold a selective stock of steel shapes, bins for shorter pieces and a small dock for sheet metal storage. Material should be classified as to metal, shape, size and length.

Ideally there should be a room for storing additional welding gas and a cabinet for moisture-proof electrode storage.

Naturally, there should be adequate tool boards in the work areas. These can be built into locked cabinets if necessary.

The storage facilities depend on the nature of the shop, the available space, the amount of work performed in the shop and the amount of stock material deemed convenient to have on hand. Often metal suppliers can give 24-hour delivery, thus reducing the necessary amount of stock in storage.

Costs

While metal is generally more expensive to use than conventional scenic materials, superior structural qualities and high reusability justify the expense. Even when its reusability is exhausted after continued theatrical service, metal still has value as scrap. The tools very often cost no more than industrial-quality woodworking equipment, and purchasing used materials, often available at scrap prices, will substantially reduce the material costs of such items as angle and pipe.

100

Bibliography and Additional Reading

Alcan Aluminum Corp. Aluminum Technical Publications. St. Louis: 1974.

Alcan Aluminum Corp. *Handbook of Aluminum.* 3d. ed. Cleveland: 1970.

American Society of Metals. "Properties, Physical Metallurgy, and Phase Diagrams." Vol. 1 of *Aluminum*, edited by Kent Van Horn. Metals Park, Ohio: 1967.

American Society of Metals. "Design and Application." Vol. 2 of *Aluminum*, edited by Kent Van Horn. Metals Park, Ohio: 1967.

American Society of Metals. "Fabrication and Finishing." Vol. 3 of *Aluminum*, edited by Kent Van Horn. Metals Park, Ohio: 1967.

American Institute of Steel Construction. *Manual of Steel Construction.* New York: 1964.

Baumeister, Theodore, ed. Marks' *Mechanical Engineers' Handbook.* 6th ed. New York: McGraw–Hill, 1964.

Benedict, Otis, Jr. *Manual of Foundry and Pattern Shop Practice.* 1st ed., 2d imp. New York: McGraw–Hill, 1947.

Bethlehem Steel Co. *Modern Steels and Their Properties.* Bethlehem, Pa.: 1964.

Blodgett, Omer W. *Design of Welded Structures.* Cleveland: James F. Lincoln Arc Welding Foundation, 1967.

Cagle, Charles V. *Adhesive Bonding, Techniques and Applications.* New York: McGraw–Hill, 1968.

Doyle, Lawrence E. *Manufacturing Processes and Materials for Engineers.* 2d ed. Englewood Cliffs, N.J.: Prentice–Hall, 1969.

Eutectic & Castolin Institute. *Gas–Tungsten Arc GTA (TIG) Manual.* Flushing, N.Y.: 1974.

Guttman, Werner H. *Concise Guide to Structural Adhesives.* New York: Van Nostrand Reinhold Co., 1961.

Hobart Trade School, *Modern Arc Welding.* Troy, Ohio.

Jefferson, T. B. *The Oxy-Acetylene Weldor's Handbook.* 6th ed. Morton Grove, Ill.: Welding Engineer Publications, 1960.

LeGrand, Rupert, ed. *The New American Machinist's Handbook*. New York: McGraw–Hill, 1955.

Lindberg, Roy A., and Braton, Norman R. *Welding and Other Joining Processes*. Boston: Allyn & Bacon, 1976.

Linde Air Products Co. *The Oxy-Acetylene Handbook*. New York: 1954.

Linde Air Products Co. *Precautions and Safe Practices*. New York, 1960.

Linde Air Products Co. *Welding and Cutting Manual*. New York, 1949.

Lipson, Charles, and Juvinall, Robert C. *Handbook of Stress and Strength*. New York: Macmillan Co., 1963.

Machine Design 39, no. 14, Reference Issue Series. "Fastening and Joining." Cleveland: Penton Publishing Co., 1967.

Machine Design 39, no. 29, Reference Issue Series. "Metals." Cleveland: Penton Publishing Co., 1967.

Meilach, Dona, and Seiden, Donald. *Direct Metal Sculpture*. New York: Crown Publishers, 1969.

Oates, J. A. *Welding Engineer's Handbook*. London: George Newnes, 1961.

Oberg, Erik, and Jones, F. D. *Machinery's Handbook*. 17th ed. New York: Industrial Press, 1964.

Parker, Harry. *Simplified Design of Structural Steel*. 3d ed. New York: John Wiley & Sons, 1965.

Parker, Harry. *Simplified Engineering for Architects and Builders*. 3d ed. New York: John Wiley & Sons, 1961.

Reynolds Metal Co. *Mechanical Fastening Methods for Aluminum*. Louisville: 1951.

Schrager, Arthur M. *Elementary Metallurgy and Metalography*. 2d ed. New York: Dover Publications, 1961.

Sullivan, R. P. *Fundamentals and Theory of Tungsten Inert Gas Art Welding*. New York: Union Carbide Corp., 1965.

United States Institute for Theatre Technology. "The Met's Turntable." *Theatre Design and Technology* 24 (February 1971).

Union Carbide Corp. *How To Do TIG (Heliarc) Welding*. New York: 1965.

Unistrut Corp. *Unistrut Metal Framing*. Catalog no. 710. Wayne, Mich.: 1964.

Untracht, Oppi. *Metal Techniques for Craftsmen*. Garden City, N.Y.: 1975.

Appendix

Wire, rod, bar, structural shapes, pipe, tube

WIRE—For WELDING, BRAZING and SOLDERING WIRE, see "Specialty Products," p. 65, this book.

 ROUND WIRE—DRAWN STRAIGHT
Length—12 ft
For diameters ⅜ in. and over, see ROD.
Coiled wire is also available in some diameters
and tempers; consult warehouse.

 **SQUARE WIRE—SHARP CORNERS,
DRAWN STRAIGHT**
Alloy 1100-H14 • Length—12 ft
For sizes ⅜ in. and over, see BAR

Other standard sizes are available from distributor and jobber stocks.

Dimension A, in.	Est wt per ft, lb	Alloy 1100-H18	Alloy 2017-T4
3/32	.008		●
1/8	.015	● ①	
5/32	.023	●	
3/16	.032	●	
1/4	.058	● ②	
5/16	.090	● ③	

① H19 temper only   ② H16 temper only   ③ H14 temper only

Dimension A, in.	Est wt per ft, lb	Alloy 1100-H14
3/16	.041	●
1/4	.073	●
5/16	.115	●

ROD

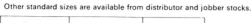 **STRAIGHT ROD**
(Diameters ⅜ in. and above are called ROD)
Other standard sizes are available from
distributor and jobber stocks.

Colored circles in columns indicate items stocked.

Dimension A, in.	Est wt per ft, lb	Alloy 6061-T651	Extruded 16-ft lengths Alloy 6063-T5	Alloy 6061-T6511
3/8	.130			
7/16	.177			
1/2	.231		●	●
9/16	.292			
5/8	.360		●	
3/4	.519		●	●
13/16	.609			
7/8	.706			●
1	.923		●	●
1-1/8	1.168			
1-1/4	1.442			●
1-3/8	1.745			
1-1/2	2.076			●
1-5/8	2.436			
1-3/4	2.826			●
1-7/8	3.244			
2	3.691			●
2-1/4	4.671			●
2-1/2	5.767			●
2-3/4	6.978			
3 ①	8.304			●
3-1/2 ①	11.303	●		
3-3/4 ①	12.975	●		
4 ①	14.763	●		
4-1/4 ①	16.666			
4-1/2 ①	18.684	●		
4-3/4 ①	20.818			
5 ①	23.067	●		
5-1/4 ①	25.432			
5-1/2 ①	27.999	●		
6 ①	33.217	●		
6-1/2 ①	38.983	●		
7 ①	45.212	●		
8 ①	59.051	●		

① Standard 12-ft lengths not available in sizes 3 in. in diameter and larger

Wire, rod, bar, structural shapes, pipe, tube

BAR

SQUARE BAR—SHARP CORNERS, EXTRUDED
ALLOY 1100-H14
For sizes under 3/8 in., see "Wire," p. 47, this book.

Dimension A, in.	Est wt per ft, lb	6063-T5(T52) 16 ft	6061-T6511 12 ft	Dimension A, in.	Est wt per ft, lb	6063-T5 16 ft	6061-T6511 12 ft
1/4	.075	●	*	2	4.800	●	
3/8	.168	●	*	2-1/4	6.076		●
1/2	.300	●	●	2-1/2	7.500		●
5/8	.468	●	●	2-3/4	9.076		●
3/4	.675	●	●	3	10.800		●
1	1.200	●	●	3-1/4	12.676		●
1-1/4	1.874	●	●	3-1/2	14.700		●
1-1/2	2.700	●	●	4	19.200		●

RECTANGULAR BAR SHARP CORNERS

Colored circles in columns indicate items stocked.

A	B	Est wt per ft, lb	Alloy 6063-T52 16-ft lengths	Alloy 6061-T6 12-ft lengths	Alloy 6061-T6511 12-ft lengths
1/8	1/2	.075	●	●	
1/8	5/8	.094	●	●	
1/8	3/4	.113	●	●	
1/8	1	.150	●	●	
1/8	1-1/4	.187	●	●	
1/8	1-1/2	.225	●	●	
1/8	1-3/4	.263	●	●	
1/8	2	.300	●	●	
1/8	2-1/2	.376	●	●	
1/8	3	.450	●	●	
1/8	3-1/2	.526	●	●	
1/8	4	.600	●	●	
3/16	1/2	.113		●	
3/16	3/4	.169	●	●	
3/16	1	.226	●	●	
3/16	1-1/4	.282	●	●	
3/16	1-1/2	.338	●	●	
3/16	1-3/4	.394	●	●	
3/16	2	.451	●	●	
3/16	2-1/2	.564	●	●	
3/16	3	.677	●	●	
1/4	1/2	.150	●		
1/4	5/8	.187	●		
1/4	3/4	.225	●		
1/4	1	.300	●	●	
1/4	1-1/4	.376	●	●	
1/4	1-1/2	.450	●	●	
1/4	1-3/4	.526	●		
1/4	2	.600	●	●	
1/4	2-1/2	.750	●	●	
1/4	3	.900	●	●	
1/4	3-1/2	1.050	●		
1/4	4	1.200	●		
5/16	3/4	.280		●	
5/16	1	.374	●	●	
5/16	1-1/4	.468		●	
5/16	1-1/2	.562	●	●	
5/16	2	.749	●	●	
5/16	3	1.123		●	
3/8	1/2	.225	●	●	
3/8	5/8	.280	●		
3/8	3/4	.337	●	●	
3/8	1	.450	●	●	
3/8	1-1/4	.564	●		
3/8	1-1/2	.675	●	●	
3/8	1-3/4	.784	●		
3/8	2	.900	●	●	
3/8	2-1/2	1.126	●		
3/8	3	1.350	●	●	
3/8	3-1/2	1.576	●		
3/8	4	1.800	●	●	
3/8	6	2.700		●	
1/2	3/4	.450	●①		●
1/2	1	.600	●①		●
1/2	1-1/4	.750	●①		●

A	B	Est wt per ft, lb	Alloy 6063-T5 16-ft lengths	Alloy 6061-T6 12-ft lengths	Alloy 6061-T6511 12-ft lengths
1/2	1-1/2	.900	●		●
1/2	1-3/4	1.050	●		●
1/2	2	1.200	●		●
1/2	2-1/2	1.500	●		●
1/2	3	1.800	●		●
1/2	3-1/2	2.100	●		●
1/2	4	2.400	●		●
1/2	5	3.000			●
1/2	6	3.600			●
5/8	1	.750	●		●
5/8	1-1/4	.937			●
5/8	1-1/2	1.124			●
5/8	2	1.500			●
3/4	1	.900	●		●
3/4	1-1/4	1.126	●		●
3/4	1-1/2	1.350	●		●
3/4	1-3/4	1.576	●		●
3/4	2	1.800			●
3/4	2-1/2	2.250			●
3/4	3	2.700			●
3/4	3-1/2	3.150			●
3/4	4	3.600			●
3/4	5	4.500			●
3/4	6	5.400			●
1	1-1/4	1.500	●		●
1	1-1/2	1.800	●		●
1	1-3/4	2.100	●		●
1	2	2.400	●		●
1	2-1/2	3.000	●		●
1	3	3.600	●		●
1	3-1/2	4.200	●		●
1	4	4.800	●		●
1	5	6.000			●
1	6	7.200			●
1-1/4	1-1/2	2.250			●
1-1/4	2	3.000			●
1-1/4	3	4.500			●
1-1/4	4	6.000			●
1-1/2	2	3.600			●
1-1/2	2-1/2	4.050			●
1-1/2	3	5.400			●
1-1/2	3-1/2	6.300			●
1-1/2	4	7.200			●
1-1/2	6	10.800			●
2	3	7.200			●
2	4	9.600			●
2	5	12.000			●
2	6	14.400			●
2-1/2	4	12.000			●
2-1/2	4-1/2	13.500			●
2-1/2	5	15.000			●
2-1/2	6	18.000			●
3	4	14.400			●
3	5	18.000			●
3	6	21.600			●

① Alloy and temper: 6063-T5

SPECIAL ANGLES, EXTRUDED

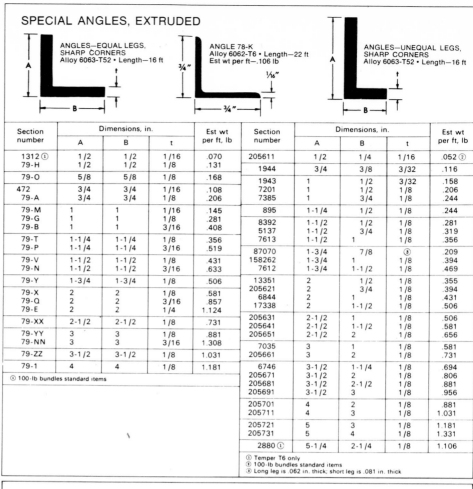

ANGLES—EQUAL LEGS, SHARP CORNERS
Alloy 6063-T52 • Length—16 ft

ANGLE 78-K
Alloy 6062-T6 • Length—22 ft
Est wt per ft—.106 lb

ANGLES—UNEQUAL LEGS, SHARP CORNERS
Alloy 6063-T52 • Length—16 ft

Section number	Dimensions, in.			Est wt per ft, lb	Section number	Dimensions, in.			Est wt per ft, lb
	A	B	t			A	B	t	
1312①	1/2	1/2	1/16	.070	205611	1/2	1/4	1/16	.052②
79-H	1/2	1/2	1/8	.131	1944	3/4	3/8	3/32	.116
79-O	5/8	5/8	1/8	.168	1943	1	1/2	3/32	.158
472	3/4	3/4	1/16	.108	7201	1	1/2	1/8	.206
79-A	3/4	3/4	1/8	.206	7385	1	3/4	1/8	.244
79-M	1	1	1/16	.145	895	1-1/4	1/2	1/8	.244
79-G	1	1	1/8	.281	8392	1-1/2	1/2	1/8	.281
79-B	1	1	3/16	.408	5137	1-1/2	3/4	1/8	.319
79-T	1-1/4	1-1/4	1/8	.356	7613	1-1/2	1	1/8	.356
79-P	1-1/4	1-1/4	3/16	.519	87070	1-3/4	7/8	③	.209
79-V	1-1/2	1-1/2	1/8	.431	158262	1-3/4	1	1/8	.394
79-N	1-1/2	1-1/2	3/16	.633	7612	1-3/4	1-1/2	1/8	.469
79-Y	1-3/4	1-3/4	1/8	.506	13351	2	1/2	1/8	.355
79-X	2	2	1/8	.581	205621	2	3/4	1/8	.394
79-Q	2	2	3/16	.857	6844	2	1	1/8	.431
79-E	2	2	1/4	1.124	17338	2	1-1/2	1/8	.506
79-XX	2-1/2	2-1/2	1/8	.731	205631	2-1/2	1	1/8	.506
79-YY	3	3	1/8	.881	205641	2-1/2	1-1/2	1/8	.581
79-NN	3	3	3/16	1.308	205651	2-1/2	2	1/8	.656
79-ZZ	3-1/2	3-1/2	1/8	1.031	7035	3	1	1/8	.581
79-1	4	4	1/8	1.181	205661	3	2	1/8	.731
					6746	3-1/2	1-1/4	1/8	.694
					205671	3-1/2	2	1/8	.806
					205681	3-1/2	2-1/2	1/8	.881
					205691	3-1/2	3	1/8	.956
					205701	4	2	1/8	.881
					205711	4	3	1/8	1.031
					205721	5	3	1/8	1.181
					205731	5	4	1/8	1.331
					2880①	5-1/4	2-1/4	1/8	1.106

① 100-lb bundles standard items

① Temper T6 only
② 100-lb bundles standard items
③ Long leg is .062 in. thick; short leg is .081 in. thick

STANDARD ANGLES①

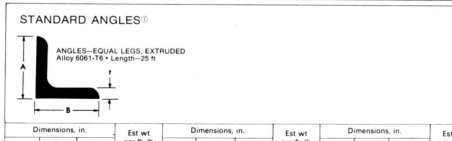

ANGLES—EQUAL LEGS, EXTRUDED
Alloy 6061-T6 • Length—25 ft

Dimensions, in.			Est wt per ft, lb	Dimensions, in.			Est wt per ft, lb	Dimensions, in.			Est wt per ft, lb
A	B	t		A	B	t		A	B	t	
3/4	3/4	1/8	.20	2	2	1/4	1.11	4	4	1/4	2.28
1	1	1/8	.28	2	2	5/16	1.36	4	4	5/16	2.83
1	1	3/16	.40	2	2	3/8	1.59	4	4	3/8	3.38
1	1	1/4	.51	2-1/2	2-1/2	1/8	.72	4	4	1/2	4.41
1-1/4	1-1/4	1/8	.35	2-1/2	2-1/2	3/16	1.07	4	4	5/8	5.42
1-1/4	1-1/4	3/16	.51	2-1/2	2-1/2	1/4	1.40	4	4	N 11/16	6.22
1-1/4	1-1/4	1/4	.66	2-1/2	2-1/2	5/16	1.73	4	4	3/4	6.83
1-1/2	1-1/2	1/8	.43	2-1/2	2-1/2	3/8	2.05	5	5	3/8	4.28
1-1/2	1-1/2	3/16	.62	3	3	3/16	1.28	5	5	1/2	5.58
1-1/2	1-1/2	1/4	.81	3	3	1/4	1.68	6	6	3/8	5.12
1-3/4	1-3/4	1/8	.51	3	3	5/16	2.08	6	6	1/2	6.75
1-3/4	1-3/4	3/16	.74	3	3	3/8	2.47	6	6	5/8	8.35
1-3/4	1-3/4	1/4	.96	3	3	1/2	3.41	8	8	1/2	9.14
2	2	1/8	.57	3-1/2	3-1/2	1/4	1.99	8	8	3/4	13.48
2	2	3/16	.85	3-1/2	3-1/2	5/16	2.46	8	8	1	17.67
				3-1/2	3-1/2	3/8	2.93				
				3-1/2	3-1/2	1/2	3.83				

① Angle sections listed as "standard" are approximations of American Standard sections. For elements of sections and detailed dimensions, consult *Alcoa Structural Handbook*.
N Not stocked at plant.

STANDARD ANGLES [1]

ANGLES—UNEQUAL LEGS, EXTRUDED
Alloy 6061-T6 • Length—25 ft

Dimensions, in. A	B	t	Est wt per ft, lb
N 1-1/4	3/4	3/32	.21
N 1-1/4	1	1/8	.31
N 1-1/2	3/4	1/8	.31
1-1/2	3/4	N 3/16	.46
N 1-1/2	1	5/32	.43
1-1/2	1	N 1/4	.66
1-1/2	1-1/4	1/8	.38
1-1/2	1-1/4	3/16	.57
1-1/2	1-1/4	1/4	.74
1-3/4	1-1/4	1/8	.42
1-3/4	1-1/4	3/16	.62
1-3/4	1-1/4	1/4	.81
2	1-1/2	1/8	.50
2	1-1/2	3/16	.73
2	1-1/2	1/4	.96
2	1-1/2	3/8	1.38
N 2-1/2	1-1/2	3/16	.85
2-1/2	1-1/2	1/4	1.11
2-1/2	1-1/2	N 5/16	1.36
2-1/2	2	1/8	.65
2-1/2	2	3/16	.96
2-1/2	2	1/4	1.26

Dimensions, in. A	B	t	Est wt per ft, lb
2-1/2	2	5/16	1.55
2-1/2	2	3/8	1.83
3	2	3/16	1.07
3	2	1/4	1.40
3	2	5/16	1.73
3	2	3/8	2.05
3	2	N 7/16	2.35
3	2-1/2	1/4	1.54
3	2-1/2	5/16	1.90
3	2-1/2	3/8	2.25
3-1/2	2-1/2	1/4	1.68
3-1/2	2-1/2	5/16	2.08
3-1/2	2-1/2	3/8	2.47
3-1/2	2-1/2	N 1/2	3.23
3-1/2	3	1/4	1.84
3-1/2	3	5/16	2.28
3-1/2	3	N 3/8	2.70
4	3	1/4	1.99
4	3	5/16	2.46
4	3	3/8	2.93

Dimensions, in. A	B	t	Est wt per ft, lb
4	3	1/2	3.83
4	3	5/8	4.69
N 4	3-1/2	3/8	3.13
4	3-1/2	N 1/2	4.10
5	3	3/8	3.35
5	3	1/2	4.40
5	3-1/2	5/16	3.01
5	3-1/2	3/8	3.58
5	3-1/2	N 7/16	4.15
5	3-1/2	1/2	4.70
5	3-1/2	5/8	5.79
6	3-1/2	5/16	3.39
6	3-1/2	N 3/8	4.04
6	3-1/2	1/2	5.31
6	4	3/8	4.24
6	4	N 7/16	4.91
6	4	1/2	5.58
6	4	5/8	6.88
6	4	3/4	8.48
N 8	6	5/8	9.84
8	6	N 11/16	10.76
8	6	3/4	11.68

[1] Angle sections listed as "standard" are approximations of American Standard sections. For elements of sections and detailed dimensions, consult *Alcoa Structural Handbook*.
N Not stocked at plant.

ZEES, EXTRUDED

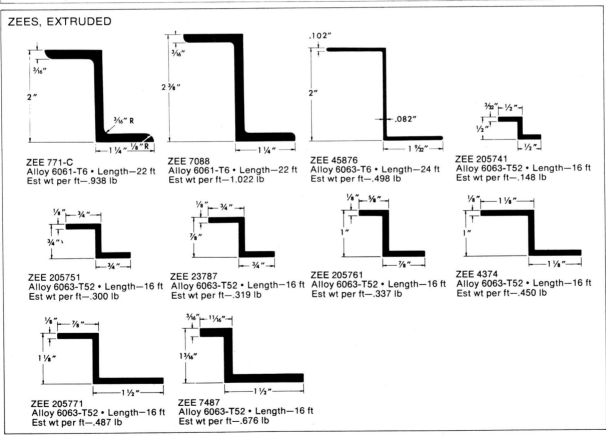

ZEE 771-C
Alloy 6061-T6 • Length—22 ft
Est wt per ft—.938 lb

ZEE 7088
Alloy 6061-T6 • Length—22 ft
Est wt per ft—1.022 lb

ZEE 45876
Alloy 6063-T6 • Length—24 ft
Est wt per ft—.498 lb

ZEE 205741
Alloy 6063-T52 • Length—16 ft
Est wt per ft—.148 lb

ZEE 205751
Alloy 6063-T52 • Length—16 ft
Est wt per ft—.300 lb

ZEE 23787
Alloy 6063-T52 • Length—16 ft
Est wt per ft—.319 lb

ZEE 205761
Alloy 6063-T52 • Length—16 ft
Est wt per ft—.337 lb

ZEE 4374
Alloy 6063-T52 • Length—16 ft
Est wt per ft—.450 lb

ZEE 205771
Alloy 6063-T52 • Length—16 ft
Est wt per ft—.487 lb

ZEE 7487
Alloy 6063-T52 • Length—16 ft
Est wt per ft—.676 lb

STANDARD STRUCTURAL ZEES, EXTRUDED

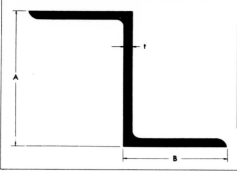

Dimensions, in.			Est area, sq in.	Max length obtainable, ft	Est wt per ft, lb
A	B	t			
2	1-1/4	3/16	0.78	50	0.94
3	2-11/16	1/4	1.98	50	2.33
4	3-1/16	1/4	2.45	85	2.88
4-1/16	3-1/8	5/16	3.04	85	3.58
4-1/8	3-3/16	3/8	3.71	85	4.36

STANDARD I-BEAMS, EXTRUDED

I-beams and H-beams sections listed as "standard" are approximations of American Standard sections. For elements of sections and detailed dimensions, consult *Alcoa Structural Handbook.*

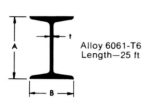

Alloy 6061-T6
Length—25 ft

Dimensions—in.			Est wt per ft, lb
A	B	t	
3	2.330	.170	1.96
3	2.509	.349	2.59
4	2.660	.190	2.64
4	2.796	.326	3.28
5	3.000	.210	3.43
5	3.284	.494	5.10

Dimensions—in.			Est wt per ft, lb
A	B	t	
6	3.330	.230	4.30
6	3.443	.343	5.10
8	4.000	.270	6.35
8	4.262	.532	8.81
10	4.660	.310	8.76
12	5.000	.350	10.99

STANDARD H-BEAMS, EXTRUDED

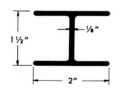

Alloy 6061-T6
Length—25 ft

Dimensions—in.			Est wt per ft, lb
A	B	t	
4	4.00	.313	4.76

SPECIAL H-BEAMS, EXTRUDED

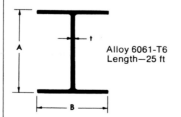

BEAM 6699
Alloy 6063-T6
Length—24 ft
Est wt per ft—.778 lb

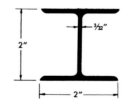

BEAM 8606
Alloy 6063-T6
Length—22 ft
Est wt per ft—.797 lb

STANDARD WIDE-FLANGE BEAMS, EXTRUDED

Alloy 6061-T6
Length—25 ft

Dimensions—in.			Est wt per ft, lb
A	B	t	
6	4	.230	4.16
6	6	.240	5.40
8	5-1/4	.230	5.90
8	6-1/2	.245	8.32
8	8	.288	10.72

Dimensions—in.			Est wt per ft, lb
A	B	t	
9.750	7.964	.292	11.41
9.900	5.750	.240	7.30
11.94	8	.294	13.84
12.06	10	.345	18.34

SPECIAL CHANNELS, EXTRUDED

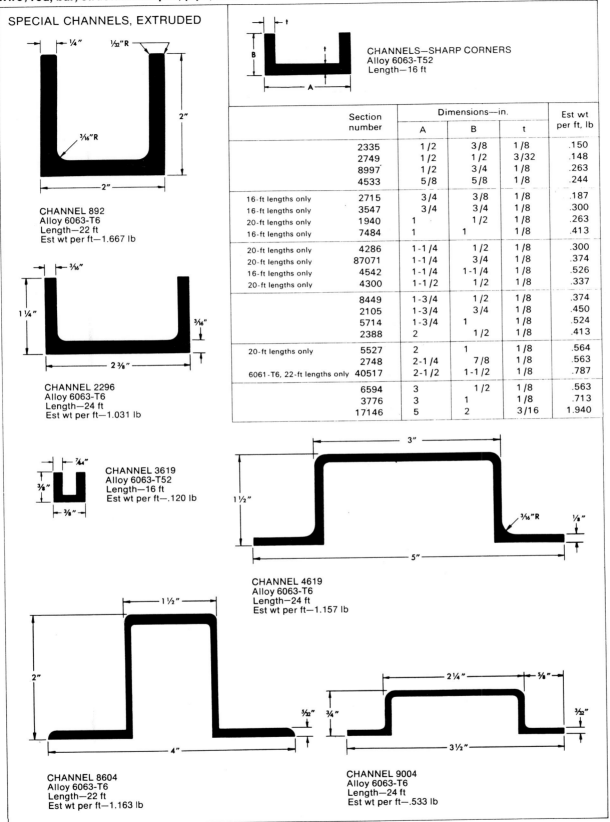

CHANNEL 892
Alloy 6063-T6
Length—22 ft
Est wt per ft—1.667 lb

CHANNEL 2296
Alloy 6063-T6
Length—24 ft
Est wt per ft—1.031 lb

CHANNEL 3619
Alloy 6063-T52
Length—16 ft
Est wt per ft—.120 lb

CHANNELS—SHARP CORNERS
Alloy 6063-T52
Length—16 ft

	Section number	Dimensions—in.			Est wt per ft, lb
		A	B	t	
	2335	1/2	3/8	1/8	.150
	2749	1/2	1/2	3/32	.148
	8997	1/2	3/4	1/8	.263
	4533	5/8	5/8	1/8	.244
16-ft lengths only	2715	3/4	3/8	1/8	.187
16-ft lengths only	3547	3/4	3/4	1/8	.300
20-ft lengths only	1940	1	1/2	1/8	.263
16-ft lengths only	7484	1	1	1/8	.413
20-ft lengths only	4286	1-1/4	1/2	1/8	.300
20-ft lengths only	87071	1-1/4	3/4	1/8	.374
16-ft lengths only	4542	1-1/4	1-1/4	1/8	.526
20-ft lengths only	4300	1-1/2	1/2	1/8	.337
	8449	1-3/4	1/2	1/8	.374
	2105	1-3/4	3/4	1/8	.450
	5714	1-3/4	1	1/8	.524
	2388	2	1/2	1/8	.413
20-ft lengths only	5527	2	1	1/8	.564
	2748	2-1/4	7/8	1/8	.563
6061-T6, 22-ft lengths only	40517	2-1/2	1-1/2	1/8	.787
	6594	3	1/2	1/8	.563
	3776	3	1	1/8	.713
	17146	5	2	3/16	1.940

CHANNEL 4619
Alloy 6063-T6
Length—24 ft
Est wt per ft—1.157 lb

CHANNEL 8604
Alloy 6063-T6
Length—22 ft
Est wt per ft—1.163 lb

CHANNEL 9004
Alloy 6063-T6
Length—24 ft
Est wt per ft—.533 lb

109

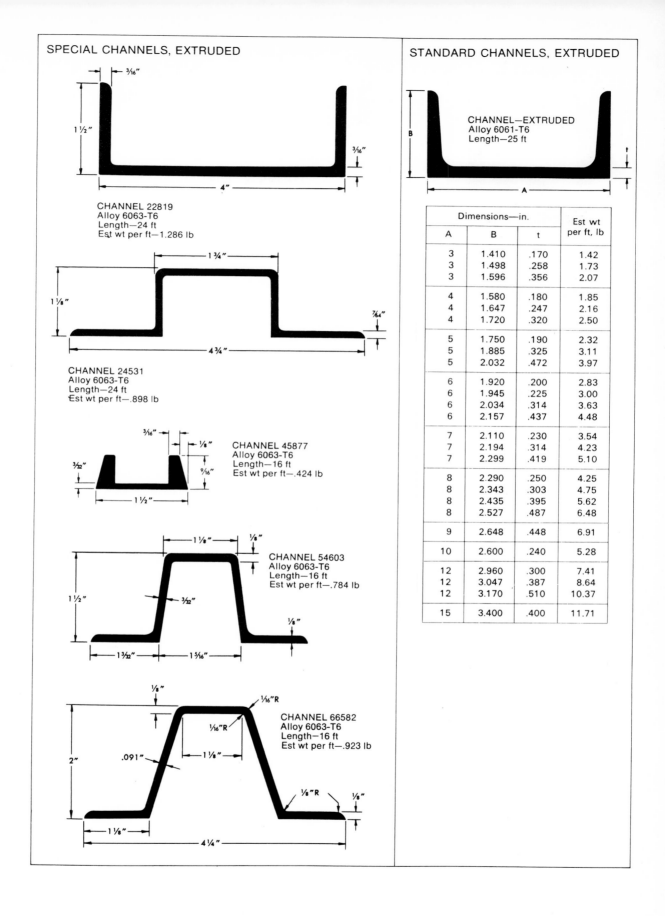

SPECIAL CHANNELS, EXTRUDED

CHANNEL 22819
Alloy 6063-T6
Length—24 ft
Est wt per ft—1.286 lb

CHANNEL 24531
Alloy 6063-T6
Length—24 ft
Est wt per ft—.898 lb

CHANNEL 45877
Alloy 6063-T6
Length—16 ft
Est wt per ft—.424 lb

CHANNEL 54603
Alloy 6063-T6
Length—16 ft
Est wt per ft—.784 lb

CHANNEL 66582
Alloy 6063-T6
Length—16 ft
Est wt per ft—.923 lb

STANDARD CHANNELS, EXTRUDED

CHANNEL—EXTRUDED
Alloy 6061-T6
Length—25 ft

Dimensions—in.			Est wt per ft, lb
A	B	t	
3	1.410	.170	1.42
3	1.498	.258	1.73
3	1.596	.356	2.07
4	1.580	.180	1.85
4	1.647	.247	2.16
4	1.720	.320	2.50
5	1.750	.190	2.32
5	1.885	.325	3.11
5	2.032	.472	3.97
6	1.920	.200	2.83
6	1.945	.225	3.00
6	2.034	.314	3.63
6	2.157	.437	4.48
7	2.110	.230	3.54
7	2.194	.314	4.23
7	2.299	.419	5.10
8	2.290	.250	4.25
8	2.343	.303	4.75
8	2.435	.395	5.62
8	2.527	.487	6.48
9	2.648	.448	6.91
10	2.600	.240	5.28
12	2.960	.300	7.41
12	3.047	.387	8.64
12	3.170	.510	10.37
15	3.400	.400	11.71

110

TEES, EXTRUDED

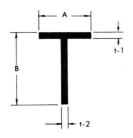

TEES—SHARP ANGLES,
SHARP CORNERS
Alloy 6063-T52
Length—16 ft

Section number	Dimensions—in.				Est wt per ft, lb
	A	B	t-1	t-2	
18307	3/4	3/4	1/8	1/8	.206
4716	3/4	1-1/4	1/8	1/8	.280
1257	1	1/2	1/8	3/8	.319
18308	1	3/4	1/8	1/8	.244
25055	1	1	1/8	1/8	.281
5951	1-1/4	7/8	1/8	1/8	.300
18906	2	3/4	1/8	1/8	.394

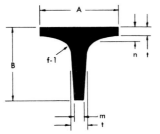

TEES—TAPER STEM AND FLANGES,
ROUNDED ANGLES, SHARP CORNERS
Alloy 6061-T6
Length—22 ft

Section number	Dimensions—in.					Est wt per ft, lb
	A x B	t	f-1	m	n	
853-F	1 x 1	1/8	1/8	5/32	5/32	.320
853-B	1-1/2 x 1-1/4	1/8	1/8	5/32	5/32	.450
853-N	1-1/2 x 1-1/4	3/16	1/8	7/32	7/32	.628
853-K	1-1/2 x 1-1/2	3/16	3/16	7/32	7/32	.700
853-G	1-1/2 x 1-1/2	1/4	3/16	9/32	9/32	.890

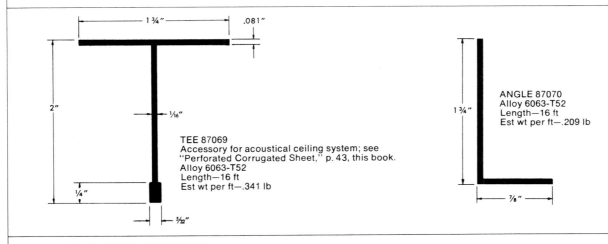

TEE 87069
Accessory for acoustical ceiling system; see
"Perforated Corrugated Sheet," p. 43, this book.
Alloy 6063-T52
Length—16 ft
Est wt per ft—.341 lb

ANGLE 87070
Alloy 6063-T52
Length—16 ft
Est wt per ft—.209 lb

STRUCTURAL TEES, EXTRUDED

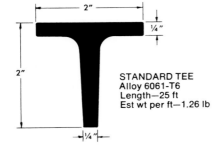

STANDARD TEE
Alloy 6061-T6
Length—25 ft
Est wt per ft—1.26 lb

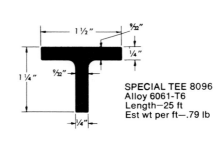

SPECIAL TEE 8096
Alloy 6061-T6
Length—25 ft
Est wt per ft—.79 lb

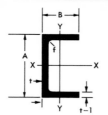

ALUMINUM ASSOCIATION STANDARD STRUCTURAL CHANNELS
Elements of sections

All dimensions in in.
Weight in lb per ft
Area in sq in.
I = Moment of inertia in in.^{4}
S = Section modulus in in.^{3}
r = Radius of gyration in in.
J = Torsion constant in in.^{4}
Cs = Torsion-bending constant in in.^{6}

Size					Area ①	Weight ②	Axis x-x			Axis y-y				J	Cs	Alcoa section
A	B	t	t₁	f			I	S	r	I	S	r	X			
2.00	1.00	.13	.13	.10	0.491	0.577	0.29	0.29	0.77	0.04	0.06	0.30	0.30	.003	0.03	292001
2.00	1.25	.17	.26	.15	0.911	1.071	0.55	0.55	0.77	0.14	0.18	0.39	0.47	.017	0.08	292011
3.00	1.50	.13	.20	.25	0.965	1.135	1.41	0.94	1.21	0.22	0.22	0.47	0.49	.011	0.31	292021
3.00	1.75	.17	.26	.25	1.358	1.597	1.97	1.31	1.20	0.42	0.37	0.55	0.62	.026	0.56	292031
4.00	2.00	.15	.23	.25	1.478	1.738	3.91	1.95	1.63	0.60	0.45	0.64	0.65	.021	1.55	292041
4.00	2.25	.19	.29	.25	1.982	2.331	5.21	2.60	1.62	1.02	0.69	0.72	0.78	.045	2.52	292051
5.00	2.25	.15	.26	.30	1.881	2.212	7.88	3.15	2.05	0.98	0.64	0.72	0.73	.033	3.97	292061
5.00	2.75	.19	.32	.30	2.627	3.089	11.14	4.45	2.06	2.05	1.14	0.88	0.95	.072	8.15	292071
6.00	2.50	.17	.29	.30	2.410	2.834	14.35	4.78	2.44	1.53	0.90	0.80	0.79	.051	8.90	292081
6.00	3.25	.21	.35	.30	3.427	4.030	21.04	7.01	2.48	3.76	1.76	1.05	1.12	.110	21.70	292091
7.00	2.75	.17	.29	.30	2.725	3.205	22.09	6.31	2.85	2.10	1.10	0.88	0.84	.057	16.90	292101
7.00	3.50	.21	.38	.30	4.009	4.715	39.79	9.65	2.90	5.13	2.23	1.13	1.20	.147	40.20	292111
8.00	3.00	.19	.35	.30	3.526	4.147	37.40	9.35	3.26	3.25	1.57	0.96	0.93	.103	34.00	292121
8.00	3.75	.25	.41	.35	4.923	5.789	52.69	13.17	3.27	7.13	2.82	1.20	1.22	.212	73.00	292131
9.00	3.25	.23	.35	.35	4.237	4.983	54.41	12.09	3.58	4.40	1.89	1.02	0.93	.131	58.20	292141
9.00	4.00	.29	.44	.35	5.927	6.970	78.31	17.40	3.63	9.61	3.49	1.27	1.25	.296	124.00	292151
10.00	3.50	.25	.41	.35	5.218	6.136	83.22	16.64	3.99	6.33	2.56	1.10	1.02	.211	102.70	292161
10.00	4.25	.31	.50	.40	7.109	8.360	116.15	23.23	4.04	13.02	4.47	1.35	1.34	.446	207.20	292171
12.00	4.00	.29	.47	.40	7.036	8.274	159.76	26.63	4.77	11.03	3.86	1.25	1.14	.371	259.60	292181
12.00	5.00	.35	.62	.45	10.053	11.822	239.69	39.95	4.88	25.74	7.60	1.60	1.61	.938	592.40	292191

① Areas listed are based on nominal dimensions.   ② Weights are based on nominal dimensions and a density of 0.098 lb per cu in. which is the density of alloy 6061.

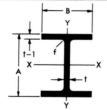

ALUMINUM ASSOCIATION STANDARD STRUCTURAL I-SHAPES
Elements of sections

All dimensions in in.
Weight in lb per ft
Area in sq in.
I = Moment of inertia in in.^{4}
S = Section modulus in in.^{3}
r = Radius of gyration in in.
J = Torsion constant in in.^{4}
Cs = Torsion-bending constant in in.^{6}

Size					Area ①	Weight ②	Axis x-x			Axis y-y			J	Cs	Alcoa section
A	B	t	t₁	f			I	S	r	I	S	r			
3.00	2.50	.13	.20	.25	1.392	1.637	2.24	1.49	1.27	0.52	0.42	0.61	0.019	1.02	292201
3.00	2.50	.15	.26	.25	1.726	2.030	2.71	1.81	1.25	0.68	0.54	0.63	0.037	1.28	292211
4.00	3.00	.15	.23	.25	1.965	2.311	5.62	2.81	1.69	1.04	0.69	0.73	0.033	3.70	292221
4.00	3.00	.17	.29	.25	2.375	2.793	6.71	3.36	1.68	1.31	0.87	0.74	0.061	4.51	292231
5.00	3.50	.19	.32	.30	3.146	3.700	13.94	5.58	2.11	2.29	1.31	0.85	0.098	12.50	292241
6.00	4.00	.19	.29	.30	3.427	4.030	21.99	7.33	2.53	3.10	1.55	0.95	0.089	25.30	292251
6.00	4.00	.21	.35	.30	3.990	4.692	25.50	8.50	2.53	3.74	1.87	0.97	0.145	29.80	292261
7.00	4.50	.23	.38	.30	4.932	5.800	42.89	12.25	2.95	5.78	2.57	1.08	0.206	63.30	292271
8.00	5.00	.23	.35	.30	5.256	6.181	59.69	14.92	3.37	7.30	2.92	1.18	0.188	106.80	292281
8.00	5.00	.25	.41	.30	5.972	7.023	67.78	16.94	3.37	8.55	3.42	1.20	0.286	123.10	292291
9.00	5.50	.27	.44	.30	7.110	8.361	102.02	22.67	3.79	12.22	4.44	1.31	0.386	223.90	292301
10.00	6.00	.25	.41	.40	7.352	8.646	132.09	26.42	4.24	14.78	4.93	1.42	0.360	339.80	292311
10.00	6.00	.29	.50	.40	8.747	10.286	155.79	31.16	4.22	18.03	6.01	1.44	0.620	406.80	292321
12.00	7.00	.29	.47	.40	9.925	11.672	255.57	42.60	5.07	26.90	7.69	1.65	0.621	894.00	234262
12.00	7.00	.31	.62	.40	12.153	14.292	317.33	52.89	5.11	35.48	10.14	1.71	1.265	1148.70	234272

Wire, rod, bar, structural shapes, pipe, tube

PIPE

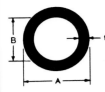

STANDARD SEAMLESS PIPE SIZE (IPS)
Length—20 ft

SCHEDULE 40 (standard)

Colored circles in columns indicate items stocked.

Nominal pipe size	Dimensions—in. A	B	t	Est wt per ft, lb	Alloys 3003-H112	3003-H18	6061-T6		6063-T6
1/8	.405	.269	.068	.085		●	●		
1/4	.540	.364	.088	.147		●	●		
3/8	.675	.493	.091	.196		●	●		
1/2	.840	.622	.109	.294		●	●		
3/4	1.050	.824	.113	.391			●		●
1	1.315	1.049	.133	.581	●		●		●
1-1/4	1.660	1.380	.140	.786	●		●		●
1-1/2	1.900	1.610	.145	.940	●		●		●
2	2.375	2.067	.154	1.264	●		●		●
2-1/2	2.875	2.469	.203	2.004	●		●		●
3	3.500	3.068	.216	2.621	●		●		●
3-1/2	4.000	3.548	.226	3.151	●		●		●
4	4.500	4.026	.237	3.733	●		●		●
5	5.563	5.047	.258	5.057	●		●		●
6	6.625	6.065	.280	6.564	●		●		●
8	8.625	7.981	.322	9.878	●		●		●
10	10.750	10.020	.365	14.006	●		●		●
12	12.750	11.938	.406	17.140	●		●		●

12-ft lengths only: 1/8 through 3/4, and 12.

Nominal pipe size	SCHEDULE 5 (featherweight) ALLOY 6063-T6 — Dimensions—in. A	B	t	Est wt per ft, lb	SCHEDULE 10 (light) ALLOY 6063-T6 — Dimensions—in. A	B	t	Est wt per ft, lb	SCHEDULE 80 (extra heavy) ALLOY 6061-T6 — Dimensions—in. A	B	t	Est wt per ft, lb
1									1.315 ①	.957	.179	.751
1-1/4					1.660	1.442	.109	.625	1.660	1.278	.191	1.037
1-1/2	1.900	1.770	.065	.441	1.900	1.682	.109	.721	1.900 ①	1.500	.200	1.256
2	2.375	2.245	.065	.555	2.375	2.157	.109	.913	2.375 ①	1.939	.218	1.737
2-1/2	2.875	2.709	.083	.856	2.875	2.635	.120	1.221				
3	3.500	3.334	.083	1.048	3.500	3.260	.120	1.498	3.500 ①	2.900	.300	3.547
3-1/2									4.000	3.364	.318	4.326
4	4.500	4.334	.083	1.354	4.500	4.260	.120	1.942	4.500 ①	3.826	.337	5.183
5	5.563	5.345	.109	2.195	5.563	5.295	.134	2.686	5.563	4.813	.375	7.188
6	6.625	6.407	.109	2.623	6.625	6.357	.134	3.214	6.625	5.761	.432	9.884
8					8.625	8.329	.148	4.637	8.625	7.625	.500	15.010

① Also available in alloy 6063-T6

TUBE

ROUND SEAMLESS TUBE—DRAWN
Length—12 ft

Colored circles in columns indicate items stocked.

Dimensions—in.		Est wt per ft, lb	Alloys and tempers	
A	t		3003-H14	6061-T6
3/16	.022	.013	●	
3/16	.035	.020		●
3/16	.049	.025		●
1/4	.022	.018	●	
1/4	.028	.023		
1/4	.035	.028	●	●
1/4	.049	.036		●
1/4	.058	.041		●
5/16	.035	.036		●
5/16	.049	.048		●
5/16	.058	.055		●
3/8	.022	.029	●	
3/8	.028	.036	●	
3/8	.035	.044	●	●
3/8	.049	.059		●
3/8	.058	.068		●
3/8	.065	.074		●
7/16	.035	.052		●
7/16	.049	.070		●
7/16	.065	.089		●
1/2	.028	.049	●	●
1/2	.035	.060	●	●
1/2	.049	.082	●	●
1/2	.058	.095	●	●
1/2	.065	.104	●	●
5/8	.028	.062	●	●
5/8	.035	.076	●	●
5/8	.049	.104	●	●
5/8	.058	.121	●	●
5/8	.065	.134	●	●
3/4	.035	.092	●	●
3/4	.049	.127	●	●
3/4	.058	.148	●	●
3/4	.065	.164	●	●
3/4	.083	.204		●
7/8	.035	.109	●	●
7/8	.049	.149	●	●
7/8	.058	.175	●	●
7/8	.065	.194	●	●
1	.035	.125	●	●
1	.049	.172	●	●
1	.058	.202	●	●
1	.065	.224	●	●
1	.083	.281		●
1	.095	.318		●
1	.125	.404		●
1-1/8	.035	.141		●
1-1/8	.049		●	
1-1/8	.058	.228		●
1-1/8	.065	.255		

Wire, rod, bar, structural shapes, pipe, tube

TUBE (continued)

ROUND SEAMLESS TUBE—DRAWN OR EXTRUDED
Length—12 ft

Colored circles in columns indicate items stocked.

Dimensions—in.		Est wt per ft, lb	Alloys and tempers	
A	t		3003-H14	6061-T6
1-1/4	.035	.157	●	●
1-1/4	.049	.217	●	●
1-1/4	.058	.256	●	●
1-1/4	.065	.284	●	●
1-1/4	.083	.357	●	●
1-3/8	.035	.173		●
1-3/8	.049			●
1-3/8	.058	.282	●	●
1-3/8	.083			●
1-1/2	.035	.189	●	●
1-1/2	.049	.263	●	●
1-1/2	.058	.309	●	●
1-1/2	.065	.344	●	●
1-1/2	.083	.434		●
1-1/2	.095			●
1-1/2	.120			●
1-1/2	.125	.635		●
1-1/2	.250	1.155		● ①
1-5/8	.035	.206		●
1-5/8	.049			●
1-5/8	.058	.336		●
1-3/4	.035	.222	●	
1-3/4	.049	.308		●
1-3/4	.058	.363		●
1-3/4	.065	.404	●	
1-3/4	.083	.510		●
1-7/8	.058	.389		●
1-7/8	.083			●
2	.035	.254	●	●
2	.049	.353	●	●
2	.058	.416		●
2	.065	.464	●	●
2	.083	.589		●
2	.125	.866		●
2	.250	1.616		● ①
2-1/4	.049	.398		●
2-1/4	.065	.520		●
2-1/4	.083	.660		●
2-1/2	.035		●	●
2-1/2	.049	.443	●	●
2-1/2	.065	.580		●
2-1/2	.083	.740		●
2-1/2	.250	2.078		● ①
3	.035		●	●
3	.049			●
3	.065	.700	●	●
3	.083	.890		●
3	.125	1.328		●
3	.250	2.540		● ①

① Extruded 6061-T 651×24 ft. lengths

TUBE (continued)

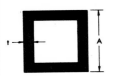

SQUARE TUBE (EXTRUDED) SHARP CORNERS
Alloy 6063-T52 • Length—21 ft, 1 in.

Dimensions, in.		Est wt per ft, lb
A	t	
3/4	.062	.205
3/4	.125	.376
1	.062	.280
1	.125	.526
1-1/4	.125	.674
1-1/2	.062	.427
1-1/2	.125	.825
1-3/4	.125	.974
2	.125	1.126
3	.125	1.726
4	.125	2.326

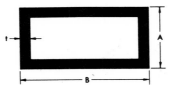

RECTANGULAR TUBE (EXTRUDED) SHARP CORNERS
Alloy 6063-T52 • Length—21 ft, 1 in.

Dimensions, in.			Est wt per ft, lb
A	B	t	
1/2	1	.125	.383
3/4	1-1/2	.125	.604
1	1-1/2	.125	.677
1	2	.125	.824
1-1/4	2-1/2	.125	1.045
1-1/2	2	.125	.971
1-3/4	3	.125	1.339
1-3/4	3-1/2	.125	1.486
1-3/4	4	.102	1.357
1-3/4	4	.125	1.633
1-3/4	4-1/2	.125	1.780
1-3/4	5	.125	1.927
2	3	.125	1.412
2	5	.125	2.000
2	6	.125	2.326
3	5	.125	2.326
3	6	.188	3.892

ROUND TUBE— HARD DRAWN, TYPE 11
Alloy 6063-T832
Length—20 ft

Dimensions, in.		Est wt per ft, lb
A	t	
3/4	.035	.092
3/4	.049	.127
3/4	.050	.148
3/4	.065	.164
7/8	.035	.109
7/8	.049	.150
7/8	.058	.175
7/8	.065	.195
1	.035	.125
1	.049	.172
1	.058	.202
1	.065	.225

Wire, rod, bar, structural shapes, pipe, tube

PIPE AND TUBE

STRUCTURAL PIPE AND TUBE—EXTRUDED
Length—20 ft

STRUCTURAL PIPE—EXTRUDED

Colored circles in columns indicate items stocked.

Nominal pipe size	Dimensions—in.		Est wt per ft, lb	Alloys	
	A	t		6061-T6	6063-T6
ASA SCHEDULE 10					
3/4	1.050	0.083	.297		●
1	1.315	0.109	.486		●
1-1/4	1.660	0.109	.625		●
1-1/2	1.900	0.109	.721		●
2	2.375	0.109	.913		●
2-1/2	2.875	0.120	1.221		●
3	3.500	0.120	1.498		●
ASA SCHEDULE 40					
1/2	0.840	0.109	.294		●
3/4	1.050	0.113	.391		●
1	1.315	0.133	.581		●
1-1/4	1.660	0.140	.786	●	●
1-1/2	1.900	0.145	.940	●	●
2	2.375	0.154	1.264	●	●
2-1/2	2.875	0.203	2.004	●	●
3	3.500	0.216	2.621	●	●
3-1/2	4.000	0.226	3.151	●	●
4	4.500	0.237	3.733	●	●
STRUCTURAL TUBE—EXTRUDED					
	1.50	0.125	.631	●	●
	1.50	0.188	.911	●	●
	....	....	1.150		
	2.00	0.125	.866	●	●
	2.00	0.188	1.260	●	●
	....	....	1.620		
	2.50	0.125	1.100		●
	2.50	0.188	1.610	●	●
	2.50	0.250	2.080		●
	3.00	0.125	1.330		●
	3.00	0.188	1.950	●	●
	3.00	0.250	2.540		
	3.50	0.125	1.560	●	●
	3.50	0.188	2.300	●	●
	3.50	0.250	3.000		
	4.00	0.125	1.790	●	●
	4.00	0.188	2.650	●	
	4.00	0.250	3.460		
	4.50	0.125	2.020	●	●
	4.50	0.188	2.990	●	●
	4.50	0.250	3.930		
	5.00	0.125	2.250		
	5.00	0.188	3.340		
	5.00	0.250	4.390		
	5.50	0.188	3.690		
	5.50	0.250	4.850		
	6.00	0.188	4.040		

WIRE AND SHEET METAL GAGES
In decimals of an inch

Name of Gage	*United States Standard Gage		The United States Steel Wire Gage	American or Brown & Sharpe Wire Gage	New Birmingham Standard Sheet & Hoop Gage	British Imperial or English Legal Standard Wire Gage	Birmingham or Stubs Iron Wire Gage	Name of Gage
Principal Use	Uncoated Steel Sheets and Light Plates		Steel Wire except Music Wire	Non-Ferrous Sheets and Wire	Iron and Steel Sheets and Hoops	Wire	Strips, Bands, Hoops and Wire	Principal Use
Gage No.	Weight Oz. per Sq. Ft.	Approx. Thickness Inches	Thickness, Inches					Gage No.
7/0's			.4900		.6666	.500		7/0's
6/0's			.4615	.5800	.625	.464		6/0's
5/0's			.4305	.5165	.5883	.432	.500	5/0's
4/0's			.3938	.4600	.5416	.400	.454	4/0's
3/0's			.3625	.4096	.500	.372	.425	3/0's
2/0's			.3310	.3648	.4452	.348	.380	2/0's
1/0			.3065	.3249	.3964	.324	.340	1/0
1			.2830	.2893	.3532	.300	.300	1
2			.2625	.2576	.3147	.276	.284	2
3	160	.2391	.2437	.2294	.2804	.252	.259	3
4	150	.2242	.2253	.2043	.250	.232	.238	4
5	140	.2092	.2070	.1819	.2225	.212	.220	5
6	130	.1943	.1920	.1620	.1981	.192	.203	6
7	120	.1793	.1770	.1443	.1764	.176	.180	7
8	110	.1644	.1620	.1285	.1570	.160	.165	8
9	100	.1495	.1483	.1144	.1398	.144	.148	9
10	90	.1345	.1350	.1019	.1250	.128	.134	10
11	80	.1196	.1205	.0907	.1113	.116	.120	11
12	70	.1046	.1055	.0808	.0991	.104	.109	12
13	60	.0897	.0915	.0720	.0882	.092	.095	13
14	50	.0747	.0800	.0641	.0785	.080	.083	14
15	45	.0673	.0720	.0571	.0699	.072	.072	15
16	40	.0598	.0625	.0508	.0625	.064	.065	16
17	36	.0538	.0540	.0453	.0556	.056	.058	17
18	32	.0478	.0475	.0403	.0495	.048	.049	18
19	28	.0418	.0410	.0359	.0440	.040	.042	19
20	24	.0359	.0348	.0320	.0392	.036	.035	20
21	22	.0329	.0317	.0285	.0349	.032	.032	21
22	20	.0299	.0286	.0253	.0313	.028	.028	22
23	18	.0269	.0258	.0226	.0278	.024	.025	23
24	16	.0239	.0230	.0201	.0248	.022	.022	24
25	14	.0209	.0204	.0179	.0220	.020	.020	25
26	12	.0179	.0181	.0159	.0196	.018	.018	26
27	11	.0164	.0173	.0142	.0175	.0164	.016	27
28	10	.0149	.0162	.0126	.0156	.0148	.014	28
29	9	.0135	.0150	.0113	.0139	.0136	.013	29
30	8	.0120	.0140	.0100	.0123	.0124	.012	30
31	7	.0105	.0132	.0089	.0110	.0116	.010	31
32	6.5	.0097	.0128	.0080	.0098	.0108	.009	32
33	6	.0090	.0118	.0071	.0087	.0100	.008	33
34	5.5	.0082	.0104	.0063	.0077	.0092	.007	34
35	5	.0075	.0095	.0056	.0069	.0084	.005	35
36	4.5	.0067	.0090	.0050	.0061	.0076	.004	36
37	4.25	.0064	.0085	.0045	.0054	.0068		37
38	4	.0060	.0080	.0040	.0048	.0060		38
39			.0075	.0035	.0043	.0052		39
40			.0070	.0031	.0039	.0048		40

* U. S. Standard Gage is officially a weight gage, in oz. per sq. ft. as tabulated. The Approx. Thickness shown is the "Manufacturers' Standard" of the American Iron and Steel Institute, based on steel as weighing 501.81 lb. per cu. ft. (489.6 true weight plus 2.5 per cent for average over-run in area and thickness). The AISI standard nomenclature for flat rolled carbon steel is as follows:

Thickness (Inches)	Width (Inches)					
	To 3½ incl.	Over 3½ To 6	Over 6 To 8	Over 8 To 12	Over 12 To 48	Over 48
0.2300 & thicker	Bar	Bar	Bar	Plate	Plate	Plate
0.2299 to 0.2031	Bar	Bar	Strip	Strip	Sheet	Plate
0.2030 to 0.1800	Strip	Strip	Strip	Strip	Sheet	Plate
0.1799 to 0.0449	Strip	Strip	Strip	Strip	Sheet	Sheet
0.0448 to 0.0344	Strip	Strip	Hot rolled sheet and strip not generally produced in these widths and thicknesses			
0.0343 to 0.0255	Strip					
0.0254 & thinner						

Appendix B

Appendix C

DECIMALS OF AN INCH
For each 64th of an inch
With Millimeter Equivalents

Fraction	1/64ths	Decimal	Millimeters (Approx.)	Fraction	1/64ths	Decimal	Millimeters (Approx.)
. . .	1	.015625	0.397	. . .	33	.515625	13.097
1/32	2	.03125	0.794	17/32	34	.53125	13.494
. . .	3	.046875	1.191	. . .	35	.546875	13.891
1/16	4	.0625	1.588	9/16	36	.5625	14.288
. . .	5	.078125	1.984	. . .	37	.578125	14.684
3/32	6	.09375	2.381	19/32	38	.59375	15.081
. . .	7	.109375	2.778	. . .	39	.609375	15.478
1/8	8	.125	3.175	5/8	40	.625	15.875
. . .	9	.140625	3.572	. . .	41	.640625	16.272
5/32	10	.15625	3.969	21/32	42	.65625	16.669
. . .	11	.171875	4.366	. . .	43	.671875	17.066
3/16	12	.1875	4.763	11/16	44	.6875	17.463
. . .	13	.203125	5.159	. . .	45	.703125	17.859
7/32	14	.21875	5.556	23/32	46	.71875	18.256
. . .	15	.234375	5.953	. . .	47	.734375	18.653
1/4	16	.250	6.350	3/4	48	.750	19.050
. . .	17	.265625	6.747	. . .	49	.765625	19.447
9/32	18	.28125	7.144	25/32	50	.78125	19.844
. . .	19	.296875	7.541	. . .	51	.796875	20.241
5/16	20	.3125	7.938	13/16	52	.8125	20.638
. . .	21	.328125	8.334	. . .	53	.828125	21.034
11/32	22	.34375	8.731	27/32	54	.84375	21.431
. . .	23	.359375	9.128	. . .	55	.859375	21.828
3/8	24	.375	9.525	7/8	56	.875	22.225
. . .	25	.390625	9.922	. . .	57	.890625	22.622
13/32	26	.40625	10.319	29/32	58	.90625	23.019
. . .	27	.421875	10.716	. . .	59	.921875	23.416
7/16	28	.4375	11.113	15/16	60	.9375	23.813
. . .	29	.453125	11.509	. . .	61	.953125	24.209
15/32	30	.46875	11.906	31/32	62	.96875	24.606
. . .	31	.484375	12.303	. . .	63	.984375	25.003
1/2	32	.500	12.700	1	64	1.000	25.400

Starrett® PRECISION TOOLS | DECIMAL EQUIVALENTS and TAP DRILL SIZES

THE L. S. STARRETT COMPANY • World's Greatest Toolmakers • ATHOL, MASSACHUSETTS, U. S. A.

FRACTION OR DRILL SIZE	DECIMAL EQUIVALENT	TAP SIZE	FRACTION OR DRILL SIZE	DECIMAL EQUIVALENT	TAP SIZE
NUMBER SIZE DRILLS 80	.0135		39	.0995	
79	.0145		38	.1015	5-40
1/64	.0156		37	.1040	5-44
78	.0160		36	.1065	6-32
77	.0180		7/64	.1093	
76	.0200		35	.1100	
75	.0210		34	.1110	6-36
74	.0225		33	.1130	6-40
73	.0240		32	.1160	
72	.0250		31	.1200	
71	.0260		1/8	.1250	
70	.0280		30	.1285	
69	.0292		29	.1360	8-32, 36
68	.0310		28	.1405	8-40
1/32	.0312		9/64	.1406	
67	.0320		27	.1440	
66	.0330		26	.1470	
65	.0350		25	.1495	10-24
64	.0360		24	.1520	
63	.0370		23	.1540	
62	.0380		5/32	.1562	
61	.0390		22	.1570	10-30
60	.0400		21	.1590	10-32
59	.0410		20	.1610	
58	.0420		19	.1660	
57	.0430		18	.1695	
56	.0465		11/64	.1719	
3/64	.0469	0-80	17	.1730	
55	.0520		16	.1770	12-24
54	.0550	1-56	15	.1800	
53	.0595	1-64, 72	14	.1820	12-28
1/16	.0625		13	.1850	12-32
52	.0635		3/16	.1875	
51	.0670		12	.1890	
50	.0700	2-56, 64	11	.1910	
49	.0730		10	.1935	
48	.0760		9	.1960	
5/64	.0781		8	.1990	
47	.0785	3-48	7	.2010	¼-20
46	.0810		13/64	.2031	
45	.0820	3-56, 4-32	6	.2040	
44	.0860	4-36	5	.2055	
43	.0890	4-40	4	.2090	
42	.0935	4-48	3	.2130	¼-28
3/32	.0937		7/32	.2187	
41	.0960		2	.2210	
40	.0980		1	.2280	
			LETTER SIZE DRILLS A	.2340	

CONTINUED ON REVERSE SIDE

Starrett PRECISION TOOLS | DECIMAL EQUIVALENTS and TAP DRILL SIZES

THE L. S. STARRETT COMPANY • World's Greatest Toolmakers • ATHOL, MASSACHUSETTS, U. S. A.

CONTINUED FROM REVERSE SIDE

FRACTION OR DRILL SIZE	DECIMAL EQUIVALENT	TAP SIZE
15/64	.2344	
B	.2380	
C	.2420	
D	.2460	
1/4	.2500	
F	.2570	5/16-18
G	.2610	
17/64	.2656	
H	.2660	
I	.2720	5/16-24
J	.2770	
K	.2810	
9/32	.2812	
L	.2900	
M	.2950	
19/64	.2968	
N	.3020	
5/16	.3125	3/8-16
O	.3160	
P	.3230	
21/64	.3281	
Q	.3320	3/8-24
R	.3390	
11/32	.3437	
S	.3480	
T	.3580	
23/64	.3594	
U	.3680	7/16-14
3/8	.3750	
V	.3770	
W	.3860	
25/64	.3906	7/16-20
X	.3970	
Y	.4040	
13/32	.4062	
Z	.4130	
27/64	.4219	1/2-13
7/16	.4375	
29/64	.4531	1/2-20
15/32	.4687	
31/64	.4844	9/16-12
1/2	.5000	
33/64	.5156	9/16-18
17/32	.5312	5/8-11
35/64	.5469	
9/16	.5625	
37/64	.5781	5/8-18

(LETTER SIZE DRILLS)

FRACTION OR DRILL SIZE	DECIMAL EQUIVALENT	TAP SIZE
19/32	.5937	11/16-11
39/64	.6094	
5/8	.6250	11/16-16
41/64	.6406	
21/32	.6562	3/4-10
43/64	.6719	
11/16	.6875	3/4-16
45/64	.7031	
23/32	.7187	
47/64	.7344	
3/4	.7500	
49/64	.7656	7/8-9
25/32	.7812	
51/64	.7969	
13/16	.8125	7/8-14
53/64	.8281	
27/32	.8437	
55/64	.8594	
7/8	.8750	1-8
57/64	.8906	
29/32	.9062	
59/64	.9219	
15/16	.9375	1-12, 14
61/64	.9531	
31/32	.9687	
63/64	.9844	1 1/8-7
1	1.0000	
1 3/64	1.0469	1 1/8-12
1 7/64	1.1093	1 1/4-7
1 1/8	1.1250	
1 11/64	1.1719	1 1/4-12
1 7/32	1.2187	1 3/8-6
1 1/4	1.2500	
1 19/64	1.2968	1 3/8-12
1 11/32	1.3437	1 1/2-6
1 3/8	1.3750	
1 27/64	1.4219	1 1/2-12
1 1/2	1.5000	

PIPE THREAD SIZES

THREAD	DRILL	THREAD	DRILL
1/8-27	R	1 1/2-11 1/2	1 47/64
1/4-18	7/16	2-11 1/2	2 7/32
3/8-18	37/64	2 1/2-8	2 5/8
1/2-14	23/32	3-8	3 1/4
3/4-14	59/64	3 1/2-8	3 3/4
1-11 1/2	1 5/32	4-8	4 1/4
1 1/4-11 1/2	1 1/2		

Credits

Drawings by Leslie Evans.

Photographs on pages 3, 5 (*top and bottom right, bottom left*), and 31 (*left*) courtesy of Terry Sateren.

Photographs on pages 7 (*top right*), 8 (*top right*), 9, and 10 (*top and bottom left*) courtesy of John Jensen.

Photograph on page 8 (*bottom right*) courtesy of Daniel Boylen.

Photograph on page 12 courtesy of Hawthorn/Olson.

Photographs on pages 7 (*bottom right*), 33, and 77 courtesy of Stuart Bratesman.

Photographs on pages 10 (*bottom right*), 42 (*top*), and 62 courtesy of Carolyn L. Ross.

Photographs on pages 4, 5 (*top left*), 6, 7 (*top and bottom left, center right*), 8 (*top and bottom left*), 10 (*top right*), 11, 18, 19, 31 (*right*), 32, 37–41, 42 (*bottom*), 43, 44, 46–48, 54, 55, 57, 59, 61, 63, 64, 67, 71, 72, 74, 75, 78, 79, 81, 85, 86, 89, 93, 95, and 100 by Douglas C. Taylor.

Book design by Madeline Bastis, Cover to Cover, Inc.
Composition by A & S Graphics, Inc.
Cover design by Marguerite Chadwick, Witworks Studio.
Printed by Noble Offset Printers, Inc.

NOTES

5110